I0826068

PRESBYTERIANISM

THREE HUNDRED YEARS AGO.

BY THE

Rev. WM. P. BREED, D.D.

PHILADELPHIA:
PRESBYTERIAN BOARD OF PUBLICATION,
No. 1334 Chestnut Street.

CONTENTS.

INTRODUCTION.

ECCLESIASTICAL history is the record of the outworking of God's decree for the world's renovation. It is the complicated story of the progress of the truth, its assaults upon error, the resistance of error to these assaults, and the results, in the life and experience of men and nations, of these onsets and oppositions—results many of them cheering and glorious, some of them fearful and bloody. Full of food for the head and the heart is such a story!

It was a wise charge, therefore, of the Presbyterian General Assembly of 1871, that its synods, presbyteries and congregations should take advantage of the advent of the year 1872 to refresh their own and the people's minds with the memories that come down to us from the year 1572, to meditate upon the furious conflicts that then were raging, to gaze again upon the grand, heroic and devoted champions that then led the hosts of Israel, and to contrast the sweet quietude of our own times with the turmoil and woes, the defeats and triumphs, of our brethren three hundred years ago. Having prepared and preached a discourse upon this subject, the writer was allured by the attractions of the theme and its obvious instructiveness to enlarge the manuscript into a small volume. There is here no pretence to original research, but simply a presentation of the results of an effort to gather and group in a brief compact form those facts which lie scattered through many volumes on our bookshelves.

The plan of the book embraces the following points:

1. A statement of the fact, together with confirmatory proof of the fact, that three hundred years ago the Protestant world was almost exclusively a Presbyterian world.

2. A rapid survey of this Presbyterian-

ism in its progress from the rise of the Reformation, and a glance at the aspect of the field three hundred years ago.

3. A glance also at the chief champions, on both sides, who figured in the conflict.

4. A narrative of some of the incidents in the great conflict of those memorable times.

We trust that the perusal of these pages may help to beget some additional interest in our Church system and history, at least in the minds and hearts of our younger Presbyterians.

PHILADELPHIA, May, 1872.

PRESBYTERIANISM.

PRESBYTERIANISM, strictly speaking, is a system of Church government, and is by no means necessarily allied to any one system of doctrine. History indeed shows it so steadily inclining toward, and so generally associated with, a certain well-known body of religious doctrine as to suggest probable affinities between them. Indeed, civil governments vary in form very largely as they vary in those fundamental doctrines respecting the natural prerogatives of manhood that severally underlie them. The general prevalence of the belief that man is made in the image of his God, and is endowed by his Creator with certain inalienable rights, is very apt to shape the civil government after some one of the various forms of Republicanism, while the doctrine of the divine right of kings will tolerate no other form of government than that of a hereditary despotism. Likewise, the system of doctrine that looks upon Adam in Eden as the legally constituted federal head and representative of the race, and the Son of God as, in like manner, the Head and Representative of all the finally saved, and that regards those finally saved as drawn to salvation through the execution of an eternal, divine decree, is perhaps, as suggested by Mr. Barnes in his essay on "The Affinities of Presbyterianism," more likely to associate itself with a system of ecclesiastical courts, with bodies for legislation and governmental control, than with the less compact system of councils for mere consultation and advice.

As a matter of history and fact, "the Presbyterian mode of government does *not* combine with Arminianism, with Sabellianism, with Pelagianism, with Socinianism; and if such a union occurs at any time, it is only a temporary and manifestly a forced connection. There are no permanent Arminian, Pelagian, Socinian presbyteries, synods, general assemblies on earth. There are no permanent instances where these forms of belief or unbelief take on the presbyterial form. There are no Presbyterian forms of ecclesiastical administration where they would be long retained."*

Still, it is none the less true that Presbyterianism, strictly speaking, is a system of Church government. It is government by an eldership. The eldership is its essential and radical idea. And it is of Presbyterianism as a form of Church government that we now write.

A Presbyterian church is a church governed by a presbytery. A presbytery consists of a body of presbyters. A presbyter is an elder. Hence any church under the governmental oversight and control of a body of elders is a Presbyterian church.

These elders are of two classes, those who, while ruling, labor also in word and doc-

* Rev. Albert Barnes.

trine, and those who rule, but labor not in word and doctrine. 1 Tim. v. 17. There are preaching elders and non-preaching elders. The preaching elders (or presbyters) stand all officially on a footing of perfect equality. The same is true of the non-preaching elders among themselves. In the governing assemblies all the elders, preaching and non-preaching, are officially equal. The vote of any one of them is of equal weight with the vote of any other.

In a thoroughly-organized Presbyterian church a certain number of non-preaching elders, elected by the people, together with the preaching elder, also elected by the people, govern a single congregation; a larger number of elders govern a cluster of congregations, and a larger number still, representing the whole Church, govern all below them.

"The radical principles of Presbyterian Church government and discipline are: That the several congregations of believers, taken collectively, constitute one Church of Christ, emphatically called the Church; that a larger part of the Church, or a representation of it, should govern a smaller or determine matters of controversy which arise therein; that in like manner a representation of the whole should govern and determine in regard to every part and to all the parts united—that is, that a majority shall govern, and consequently that appeals may be carried from lower to higher judicatories till they be finally decided by the collected wisdom and united voice of the whole Church."

Thus in a Presbyterian church "the people have a right to a substantive part in its government; presbyters who minister in word and doctrine are the highest permanent officers of the Church and all belong to the same order, and the outward and visible Church is or should be one in the sense that a smaller part is subject to a larger and a larger to the whole." This is Presbyterianism.

I.

PRESBYTERIANISM THREE HUNDRED YEARS AGO.

THREE hundred years ago the Protestant world was almost exclusively a Presbyterian world. The early Reformers, as is well known to all familiar with the history of their times, when they put off the tyranny of Rome, adopted, almost with one consent, the fundamental principles of Presbyterianism—namely, official equality among the clergy and government by presbyterial bodies. To this the Church of England, that owes its origin to Henry VIII., was almost the sole exception.

1. For antiquity, for purity of doctrine, and for fidelity in keeping and for zeal in propagating the faith once delivered to the saints, the Church of the Waldenses stands in the very front rank. And this Church was a Presbyterian Church.

"As early as the sixteenth century," writes Dr. Smythe, with abundant learning and a profuse array of quotations from various authorities, "the Waldensian polity was precisely what it is now. Every church had its consistory, every consistory and pastor was subject to the synod, and it was composed of all the pastors, with elders. Over this synod one of the ministers was chosen by his brethren, and without any second ordination presided. This presiding minister was called *then*, as he is called *now*, moderator. He was required, in accordance with the plan of the early Scottish Church, to visit different parishes, and to ordain *only in conjunction* with other ministers. But he was in all things responsible to the synod by which he had been appointed to office."

Milner (vol. ii., chap. iii.) quotes the following from a book concerning the Waldensian pastors: "The pastors meet once every year to settle our affairs in a general synod. The money given us by the people is carried to the said general synod, and is there received by the elders."

2. As to the mother of the Reformed Churches, at Geneva, Mosheim writes: "Calvin introduced into the republic of Geneva, and endeavored to introduce into all the Reformed Churches throughout Europe, that form of ecclesiastical government which is called Presbyterian, from its admitting neither the institution of bishops nor of any subordination among the clergy. He established at Geneva a consistory composed of ruling elders, partly pastors and partly laymen, and invested this ecclesiastical body with a high degree of authority. He also convened synods composed of ruling elders of different churches, and in these had laws enacted for the regulation of all matters of a religious nature."

3. Not one whit behind any Church of the Reformation in the thoroughness of its Presbyterianism was the Church of France. In the Confession of Faith drawn up in Paris in 1559, we read:

"Article xxix. We believe that this true Church ought to be governed by that discipline which our Lord Jesus hath established, so that there should be in the Church pastors, elders and deacons, that the pure doctrine may have its course and vices may be reformed and suppressed.

"Article xxx. We believe that all true pastors, in whatever places they may be disposed, have all the same authority and equal power among themselves under Jesus Christ, the only Head, the only Sovereign and only universal Bishop."

As to the type of Presbyterianism that obtained in France, Dr. Hodge, in his Constitutional History of the Presbyterian Church in the United States, writes: "It is a great mistake to suppose that French Presbyterianism was more mild than that of Scotland. There are many acts of her synods which would make modern ears tingle, and which prove that American Presbyterianism in its strictest forms was a sucking dove compared to that of the immediate descendants of the

Reformers." Some idea of the kind of Presbyterianism which prevailed in France may be gathered from the fact that the provincial synods were obliged to furnish their deputies to the national synod with a commission in these terms:

"We promise before God to submit ourselves unto all that shall be concluded and determined in your holy assembly, to obey and execute it to the utmost of our power, being persuaded that God will preside among you and lead you by his Holy Spirit into all truth and equity by the rule of his word, for the good and edification of his Church, to the glory of his great name, which we humbly beg of his divine Majesty in our daily prayers."

4. The Church of Holland was twin sister in doctrine and discipline with the Church of France.

"The Reformation," writes Motley, "entered Holland through the 'Huguenot Gate.' It may safely be asserted," he adds, "that the early Reformers of the provinces were mainly Huguenots in their belief." How safely this may be asserted is seen in the fact that "when the deputies from the Dutch churches appeared in the national synod (of France) held in 1583, and tendered the Confession of Faith and body of church discipline owned and embraced by the said churches of the Low Countries, this assembly, having humbly and heartily blessed God for that secret union and agreement, both in doctrine and discipline, between the churches of this kingdom and that republic, did judge meet *to subscribe them both;* and it did also request those, our brethren, their deputies, reciprocally to subscribe our Confession of Faith and body of church discipline, which in obedience to the commission given them by their principals they did accordingly, thereby testifying mutual harmony and concord in doctrine and discipline of all the churches in both nations."*

5. In the Lutheran Church, also, we find the fundamental principles of Presbyterian-

* Hodge's "Constitutional History."

ism. The Rev. Dr. S. S. Schmucker quotes of the early Lutheran emigrants to America: "They at once adopted the form which Luther and the Lutheran divines generally have always regarded as the primitive one—viz., the parity of ministers, the co-operation of the laity in church government and the free voluntary convention of synods."

"The doctrine of Presbytery as opposed to Prelacy," writes Dr. Wm. Cunningham in his Historical Theology, "was not only held, as we have seen, by Luther and his associates, but was distinctly declared in the Articles of Schmalkalden, which is one of the symbolical books of the Lutheran Church. There it is set forth that all the functions of church government belong equally of right to all who preside over churches, whether called pastors, presbyters or bishops; and this general principle is expressly applied to ordination, as proving that ordination by ordinary pastors is valid."

As to the superintendents in some of the Lutheran churches, "this institution affords no testimony in favor of proper prelacy. These superintendents are not regarded as holding a distinct higher office, superior to that of presbyters, and investing them simply as holding that office with jurisdiction over ordinary pastors, but merely as presbyters raised by the common consent of their brethren to a certain very limited control for the sake of order. This institution is no proof that the Lutheran Church hold the doctrine of prelacy, but merely that they hold the lawfulness of a certain limited pre-eminence or superiority being conferred by presbyters upon one of themselves."

Even the ecclesiastical government in Denmark, Sweden and Norway shows "but a slight deviation from the general uniformity of the Reformed Churches as a whole; and, besides, the Protestant bishops set up in these countries at the Reformation were not the regular successors of men who had been consecrated to the episcopal office, but derived their ordination and authority from

Luther and the presbyters who were associated with him."

6. That in England the great body of the early Reformers who refused submission to the exactions of Henry VIII. and Elizabeth were Presbyterians in principle is abundantly evident.

It is perhaps a common impression that the term Puritan, as applied to the early English dissenters, was in the ecclesiastical view generally synonymous with the term Independent. This is very wide of the truth. Mingled with the English Reformers was a large number of Independents who did good service in the fight for liberty of worship, but they were far outnumbered by the Presbyterians.

As for Wickliffe, the morning star of the Reformation, he was for "rejecting *all* human rites, and with regard to the identity of the order of bishops and priests in the apostolic age he was very positive." On the essential points of Presbyterianism the opinion of distinguished clergymen in the early Church of England is very significant. Even Cranmer proposed the erection of courts similar to the kirk sessions and provincial synods afterward introduced into the Church of Scotland and universal among the Presbyterians of the Continent.

When, in 1588, Bancroft, chaplain to the archbishop, in a sermon at St. Paul's Cross, broached the novelty "that the bishops of England were a distinct order from the priests, and had superiority over them by divine right and directly from God," Whitgift, the learned and zealous prelatist, said that "he rather wished than believed it to be true."

Dr. John Reynolds, regarded at that time as the most learned man in the Church of England, in an answer to this sermon of Bancroft, wrote:

"*All who have for five hundred years last past endeavored the reformation of the Church have taught that all pastors, whether they be called bishops or priests, are invested with equal authority and power*, as first the Waldenses, next Marsilius Patavianus, then Wickliffe and his scholars, afterward Huss and the Hussites, and last of all Luther, Calvin, Brentius, Bullinger and Musculus. Among ourselves we have bishops, the queen's professors of divinity in our universities and other learned men consenting therein, as Bradford, Lambert, Jewel, Pilkington, etc. But why do I speak of particular persons? It is the common judgment of the Reformed churches of Helvetia, Savoy, France, Scotland, Germany, Hungary, Poland, the Low Countries *and our own.*"

The "Discipline of the Church as described in the word of God," drawn up by Travers and printed at Geneva, 1574, which is thoroughly Presbyterian, was afterward subscribed by more than *five hundred beneficed clergymen in England* as agreeable to the word of God and to be promoted by all lawful means. Neal writes that under the reigns of Elizabeth and James I. the Puritans were for the most part Presbyterians, and at the restoration of Charles II. he says that the Presbyterians were in possession of the whole power of England; the council of state, the chief officers of the army and navy and the governors of the chief forts and garrisons were theirs. Their clergy were in possession of both universities and of the best livings in the kingdom.

7. Of the Presbyterianism of Scotland, shaped under the eye and largely by the hand of Knox, we need not speak.

Thus, at the Reformation, the Church by almost unanimous consent flew back, as a child escaped from the wilderness to its mother's bosom, to Presbyterianism, and three hundred years ago the Protestant world was almost exclusively a Presbyterian world.

II.

THE FIELD.

LET us now take a rapid survey of Presbyterianism in its progress from the rise of the Reformation, and in its actual condition as to organization and the number of its adherents in 1572.

PIEDMONT.

In seeking for Presbyterianism in 1572, it seems strange that we should have to spend a thought on Rome-ridden Italy. And yet it is to Italy we betake ourselves in quest of the oldest body of Presbyterians in the wide world!

In the extreme north-west of that sunny land, separating Italy from France, there rises a pile of mountain barriers whose snowy peaks look down upon the clouds. This mountain mass forms the western side of an almost triangular patch of territory, hemmed in by mountains on the north and mountains on the south, and sloping down and narrowing as it falls toward the sunny plains of Piedmont upon the east. This area is ridged with rough, angular, precipitous mountains, ploughed with deep, steep-sided, secluded glens, with easier slopes here and there that afford precarious herbage for the chamois and sustenance more meagre and precarious for man.

Sweeping down from the north-west to the south-east is one deep valley, called Pragela in part of its extent and farther on Perouse. South of this, and opening into it just where the Pragela ends and the Perouse begins, is the valley of St. Martin. On the southern side of the triangle, and running almost directly eastward, is the valley of Luserne, and opening into it from the north the valley of Angrogna, and from the south another deep secluded valley, that of Rosa.

Through these valleys, rugged with rocky fragments that have plunged down their steep sides from the awful overhanging cliffs, rush impetuous mountain torrents which sometimes overflow their banks and with resistless fury sweep away cattle, people and houses. All along their sides deep clefts in the mountains discharge into them their contributions of melted snows in foaming streams. Here and there at a dizzy height juts out a stupendous mountain crag which flings a huge shadow on the valley below. The land abounds in chasms, grottoes and caves. In the great crag of Casteluzzo, in the valley of Luserne, there is a vast natural grotto, scooped out and cleared till it is capable of containing upward of three hundred persons. Through the clefts of the rock sufficient light makes its way and an approaching foe may be observed. The entrance to it is by a tunnel just large enough to admit one person at a time. Here and there the valley narrows into a mere gorge along whose sides a path affords precarious footing for the traveler, while over his head projecting cliffs threaten destruction. In many portions of this wild country the pastor wears clogs under his shoes, the soles and heels of which are studded with spikes more than an inch long, to make it tolerably safe to move about in winter among the people of his flock. Far up the valley of Angrogna is the Pra del Tor, the "Meadow of the Tower," the ancient seat of a Waldensian theological school. It is a narrow defile hemmed in by steep and inaccessible rocks which form a sublime natural circumvallation of the spot. The eyrie of the eagle is hardly more secure from hostile intrusion.

Interspersed amid all this ruggedness are spots of comparative fertility, yet in the deeper recesses the harvest is meagre and sometimes the unreaped fields are swept to desolation by furious avalanches. Farther down toward the plain the lands are richer and more productive.

Now, all this rugged land, from its lower, sunnier slopes to its deepest, darkest caverns, its awful mountain gorges, its dizzy terraces, its every foot is hallowed ground! No deep recess but has echoed now with the preacher's impassioned voice, the sounds of prayer and praise, and now with the wail of woe. Everywhere its soil has been pressed and its soilless rocks worn by the knees of the suppliant pleading in Jesus' dear name. Yes, and wild shrieks of martyred men, women and children have drowned the sounds of avalanche and mountain torrent there, and those turbid glacier streams have again and again been crimsoned with martyrs' blood!

In days far back almost as the times of the apostles, out from their quiet homes on the sunny plains below, up into those deep, cold, dark recesses, the poor persecuted saints were driven, bearing with them the form and institutions of the faith delivered to the saints by Christ and the apostles.

So early as 1520, Romish historians represent the dwellers in these valleys as forming the most ancient of heretical sects. One of their own historians, writing near the close of the seventeenth century, says, "The Waldenses are descended from those refugees who, after St. Paul had there preached the gospel, abandoned their beautiful country and fled, like the woman mentioned in the Apocalypse, to these wild mountains, where they have to this day handed down the gospel from father to son in the same purity and simplicity as it was preached by St. Paul." And right pertinent is the question, "Is it wonderful if the glare of the fires at Rome, where Christians were bound to stakes, covered with pitch and burnt in the evenings to illuminate the city, should induce those yet at liberty to betake themselves for shelter to the almost inaccessible valleys of the Alps and to the clefts of the rocks, trusting to that God in whose hands are the deep places of the earth, and considering that the strength of the hills is his also?"

To the Reformer Œcolampadius and others the Waldenses in 1530 wrote: "That you may at once understand the matter, we are a sort of teachers of a certain necessitous and small people, who already, for more than four hundred years—nay, as those of our country frequently relate, *from the times of the apostles*—have sojourned among the most cruel thorns, yet, as all the pious have easily judged, not without great favor of Christ."

Hence, welcoming the name *evangelical*, they indignantly refuse the name "Protestant" in the modern sense of the word. For having never submitted to the impostures of Rome, they were never called upon to reject them.

The story of their sorrows at one time thrilled all Europe and drew from Milton's sublime pen the noted adjuration:

"Avenge, O Lord! thy slaughtered saints whose bones
Lie scattered on the Alpine mountains cold;
Even them who kept thy truth so pure of old,
When all our fathers worshiped stocks and stones—
Forget not, in thy book record their groans
Who were thy sheep, and in their ancient fold
Slain by the bloody Piedmontese that rolled
Mother with infant down the rocks. Their moans
The vales redoubled to the hills, and they

> To heaven. Their martyred blood and ashes sow
> O'er all the Italian fields where still doth sway
> The triple tyrant, that from these may grow
> A hundredfold who, having learned thy way,
> Early may fly the Babylonian woe."

In that northern valley of Pragela on Christmas day, 1400, a furious onset was made upon the faithful by the devotees of the pope. Many were slain; and as the snow was deep, the escaping fugitives perished by the way, and on the following morning some eighty infants were found dead beside their dying mothers.

In 1500 the valley of Luserne was made to run with Vaudois blood. Very many of the persecuted people died in prison, whilst some were burned alive.

Near La Tour, at the junction of the valleys of Angrogna and Luserne, deeds were done that shame the human name. Houses and churches were burned to the ground; infants were torn from their mothers' breasts and dashed against the rocks; the sick were either burned alive, cut in pieces or rolled down precipices with their head and feet tied together; many had gunpowder crammed into the mouth and exploded; multitudes were mutilated in various ways—nose, fingers and toes cut off—and then turned out to perish in the snow. Other deeds were done too shameless to record.

How piteously and piously did they plead for relief from the horrors of persecution, and yet with what firm fidelity to the truth! Ten or twelve years before 1572 they addressed a petition to Philibert Emmanuel, duke of Savoy and prince of Piedmont, in which they say:

"We do protest before the almighty and all-just God, before whose tribunal we must all one day appear, that we intend to live and die in the holy faith, piety and religion of our Lord Jesus Christ, and that we do abhor all heresies that have been and are condemned by the word of God.

"We do embrace the most holy doctrines of the prophets and apostles, as likewise of the Nicene and Athanasian creeds; we subscribe to the four councils and to all the ancient Fathers in all such things as are not repugnant to the analogy of faith.

"The Turks, Jews, Saracens and other nations, though never so barbarous, are suffered to enjoy their own religion, and we who serve and worship in faith the true and almighty God and one true and only Sovereign, the Lord Jesus, and confess one God and one baptism, shall not we be suffered to enjoy the same privileges?

"We humbly implore your Highness' goodness, and that for our only Lord and Saviour Jesus Christ's sake, to allow unto us, your most humble subjects, the most holy gospel of the Lord our God in its purity, and that we may not be forced to do things against our consciences."

The Church polity of this people, as has already been shown, is now and has been as far back as memory reaches, in all essential points, Presbyterian.

"They have in each congregation a consistory equivalent to the church session. The consistory is composed of the pastor, the elders and the deacons. The deacons have the care of the poor. The elders are first nominated by the congregation and then elected by the consistory. They are regularly installed after sermon in the church, and have a charge to watch over the spiritual interests of the flock, to aid the pastor, to reprove the erring, to exhort to the performance of duty, and two of them are appointed to represent the congregation in the higher ecclesiastical tribunal. The Waldenses believe in the parity of the ministry, their pastors, or *barbas,* being all equal. They have ecclesiastical supervision by a court of review and control. They have but one superior ecclesiastical court—viz., the synod—which includes the functions of both presbytery and synod. The synod is composed of all the ministers who are actual pastors or professors in their colleges, and of two elders from each parish, who, however, have but one vote. The synod elect one of their ministers as moderator, whose office continues till the time of the next meeting. His office gives him no power beyond that of any presiding officer, and it expires with the appointment of his successor. The ceremony of ordination with them is precisely similar to the corresponding rite as it is practiced in the Presbyterian Church of the United States."

In 1572 we find this people, for so many centuries the bush burning in the fires of persecution, yet unconsumed, still nestling in their mountain recesses, with the snow-peaked heights towering above them, the crash of the avalanche and the hiss and roar of the glacier torrents ever in their ears, and a wicked, wily and remorseless foe ever ready to spring with tiger ferocity upon them. Of their actual numbers three hundred years ago it is impossible to speak with certainty. That, however, they formed a pretty numerous body is evident from the numbers which were constantly given of the slaughtered and imprisoned in the various persecuting onslaughts made upon them.

SWITZERLAND.

Crossing the mountain barriers that encompass the sighing valleys and gorges of the Waldenses, we find ourselves in Switzerland.

"The history of the Swiss Reformation," writes D'Aubigné, "is divided into three periods in which the light of the gospel is seen spreading successively over three different zones. From 1519 to 1526, Zurich was the centre of the Reformation, which was then entirely German, and was propagated in the eastern and northern parts of the Confederation. Between 1526 and 1532 the movement was communicated from Berne, which is at once German and French, and extended to the centre of Switzerland, from the gorges of the Jura to the deepest valleys of the Alps. In 1532, Geneva became the focus of light, and the Reformation, which was here essentially French, was established on the Leman Lake and gained strength in every quarter."

For centuries Switzerland was the stronghold of the papacy; it is to become one mountain-girt fortification of a purified Christianity. Mont Blanc rises not more grandly from Chamouny than is Swiss Presbyterianism to rise before the eyes of Europe.

When the sounds from the gospel trumpet began to reverberate among the mountains of Switzerland, the world wondered at the host of champions that at once responded to the summons.

FAREL came—the almost rashly intrepid Farel, the man who, encountering a Romish procession in honor of St. Anthony, felt his spirit so stirred within him that he seized the image of the saint and threw it into the river! Journeying from Strasburg to Switzerland in company with a single friend, night closed around them, the rain fell in torrents, and the travelers, in despair of finding their road, had sat down midway, drenched with rain. "Ah!" said Farel, "God, by showing me my helplessness in these little things, has willed to teach me what I am in the greatest, without Jesus Christ." At last, springing up, he plunged into the marshes, waded through the waters, crossed vineyards, fields, hills, forests and valleys, and at length reached his destination.

"Let us scatter the seed everywhere," writes this evangelical Jehu, "and let civilized France, provoked to jealousy by this barbarous nation, embrace piety at last. Let there not be in Christ's body either fingers or hands or feet or eyes or ears or arms existing separately and working each for itself, but let there be only one heart that nothing can divide." In his preaching he seemed to thunder rather than speak. They rang the bells to drown his voice and drew their swords to intimidate him, and all equally in vain.

Œcolampadius, the *Melanchthon* of Switzerland, appeared. He was as meek and quiet as Farel was impetuous. His books were his bosom friends. Tall, handsome, patriarchal in appearance, his influence in

Switzerland was second in weight only to that of Zwingle or Calvin.

ULRICH ZWINGLE is another name that will be known and honored as long as any of those inscribed upon the walls of the restored Church in Switzerland. Twenty miles from the south-eastern extremity of Lake Zurich, and two thousand feet above the level of the lake, there was a small village named Wildhaus. "The fruits of the earth grew not upon these heights. A green turf of Alpine freshness ascends the sides of the mountain, above which enormous masses of rock rise in savage grandeur to the skies." Here is a pleasant cottage "of thin walls, windows composed of round panes of glass, roof formed of shingles loaded with stones to prevent their being carried away by the wind. Before the house bubbles a limpid stream."

In this lonely chalet, occupied by a family of the name of Zwingle, on New Year's day, 1484, seven weeks after the birth of Luther, a babe was born and named Ulrich.

As he grew up, the boy was sent to study at Berne, and having there become familiar with polite letters, went thence to Vienna to acquaint himself with philosophy. Again, at the age of eighteen, we find him at Basle, a teacher in St. Martin's school and a student of scholastic divinity, until, weary with its babbling, confused inanities, he cast it from him in disgust. At the age of twenty-two he became priest of Glaris, not far from his native place. The spirit in which he entered upon his work at this place is disclosed in his own words: "Young as I was, the office of the priesthood filled me with greater fear than joy, for this was ever present to me—that the blood of the sheep who perished through any neglect or guilt of mine would be required at my hands."

To equip himself for the solemn work before him, the young priest devoted himself with all ardor to the study of the New Testament. Paul's Epistles he copied in Greek with his own hand, filling the margin with observations of his own and with quotations from the Fathers.

From Glaris, Zwingle went to Einsidlen. Here he committed to memory the Epistles of St. Paul and afterward other books of the Old and New Testaments. Here he obtained still deeper insight into the knavery of the Church of Rome and the wrongs it inflicted on the people, and according to his ever-increasing light his preaching became more clear and evangelical. Here his education as Reformer was completed.

And now Zurich called him—"cheerful, animated" Zurich, with its amphitheatre of hills covered with vineyards or adorned with pastures and orchards and crowned with forests above which appear the highest summits of the Alps. Zurich, the centre of the political interests of Switzerland, and in which were often collected the most influential men in the nation, was the spot best adapted for acting on Helvetia and scattering the seeds of truth through all the cantons. Accordingly, the friends of learning and of the Bible joyfully hailed Zwingle's nomination.

Now began the great work and struggle of his life. It was on Saturday, the first day of the year 1519, Zwingle's thirty-fifth birthday, that he entered the pulpit of the cathedral church of Zurich—a pulpit that for centuries had spoken only in the name of the pope of Rome. Among his first words in that pulpit were these: "It is to Christ that I desire to lead you—to Christ, the true source of salvation. His divine word is the only food that I wish to set before your hearts and souls." The crowds came together to hear his expositions of the Gospels. The common people listened to him gladly. "Bold and energetic in the pulpit, he was affable to all that he met in the streets or public places," and thus he won the hearts as well as instructed the minds of the people.

In 1523 he secured the gathering of an assembly at Zurich and the passage of an edict which made the doctrines of the Reformation the largely accepted doctrines of the whole canton. In 1527, in a much larger assembly at Berne, Zwingle and others discussed the great doctrines of the gospel and mightily convinced many halting ones. As a result, Berne adopted the Reformed worship, and in less than four months all the municipalities of the canton followed its example.

HENRY BULLINGER, too, heard and answered the reforming call. When three years old he would find his way into the church, climb into the pulpit and recite the Lord's Prayer and the Apostles' Creed. When a boy at school, like Luther, he gained his bread by singing songs from door to door. At the age of sixteen he found and opened the New Testament, and there, said he, "I found all that is necessary for man's salvation." From that time the Fathers were nothing to him, but he explained Scripture by Scripture, as the Scriptures themselves command and the pope forbids. He acquired vast stores of learning, was one of the authors of the Helvetic Confession, and assisted Calvin in drawing up the formulary of 1549. He was a faithful, conscientious man, and one of the bulwarks of the Reformation. He was the successor of Zwingle at Zurich.

Writes D'Aubigné: "The youthful Henry Bullinger, threatened with the scaffold, had been compelled to flee from Bremgarten, his native town, with his aged father, his colleague and sixty of the principal inhabitants. Three days after this he was preaching in the cathedral of Zurich. "No, Zwingle is not dead!" exclaimed Myconius, "or, like the phœnix, he has risen again from his ashes." Bullinger was unanimously chosen to succeed the great Reformer. He adopted Zwingle's orphan children, and endeavored to supply the place of their father. This young man, then scarce twenty-eight years of age, and who presided forty years with wisdom and blessing over this church, was everywhere greeted as the apostle of Switzerland.

Among this school of worthies was OSWALD MYCONIUS. He was a native of Lucerne. His youthful eyes often glanced over the Lake of the Four Forest Cantons to the Rigi, and often up to the cloudy peak of Mount Pilatus. He was a schoolmaster, and at the same time a disciple of Him who said, "Learn of me." He taught at Berne and then at Basle. In 1516 he withdrew from Basle to become the superintendent of the cathedral church at Zurich. There, while he gave lessons in literature, he failed not to teach the unsearchable riches of Christ, declaring that "if the pope and the emperor command anything in opposition to the gospel, man is bound to obey God alone, who is above both the emperor and the pope."

It was largely through the efforts and influence of Myconius that Zwingle came to Zurich. There, for a time, they two walked together arm in arm and fought together shoulder to shoulder. But a call came from his native land. He was made head-master of the collegiate school at Lucerne. At his departure Zwingle was in great sorrow. "Your departure," he wrote, "has inflicted a blow on the cause I am defending like that suffered by an army when one of its wings is destroyed." Poor, faithful Myconius! Lucerne papists drove him and his feeble wife and child into exile, but God reaped a harvest from the seed he sowed.

Francis Lambert also appeared. He was a Franciscan friar who lived at Avignon. As soon as his neighbors began to take knowledge of him that he had been with Jesus they threatened him, and he fled to Geneva, where he preached the gospel; then crossing the lake, he climbed the hill and preached the gospel at Lausanne; next we find him where the rushing Sarine washes the bases of the heights of Freyburg, and the citizens of Berne listen to him while he denounces the mass, the traditions of Romanism and the superstitions and vices of the monks. There he goes in his monk's dress, riding on an ass, his legs so long that his bare feet almost touch the ground, on, on through narrow ravines, along dizzy precipices, over mountains and across the vales. He comes to Zurich, preaches four sermons, in one of which, his eyes but partially opened, he speaks with commendation of praying to the Virgin and the saints.

A voice from the congregation calls out, "Brother, you are mistaken!" It is the voice of Zwingle.

Lambert challenges Zwingle to a public disputation of the point. Zwingle promptly accepts. Great is the excitement in Zurich. What sadder to the believers, what more delightful to the papists, than a quarrel between the Reformers!

A large assembly gathered. Zwingle spoke long and with great power, showing the folly and the sin of praying to the saints and the Virgin. Lambert's turn came to reply. Standing up, he clasped his hands together, raised his eyes to heaven and exclaimed:

"I thank thee, O God! that by means of this great and good servant of thine thou hast brought me to a fuller knowledge of the truth." Then turning to the people, he added, "Henceforth in all my troubles I will call upon God alone, and I will throw aside my beads."

The next day he left Zurich, mounted on his ass, first visiting Erasmus at Basle, and afterward Luther at Wittenberg.

Another champion of the faith in Switzerland was THOMAS WITTEMBACH. In 1505 he preached in Basle. He was earnest, of sincere piety, skilled in the liberal arts and in mathematics, and profound in his knowledge of the word of God. His lectures kindled a deep interest in many waiting hearts. Zwingle was among the charmed listeners to his words. "The hour is not far distant," said the lecturer, "in which the scholastic theology will be set aside and the old doctrines of the Church revived. Christ's death is the only ransom for our souls."

Among those listeners to the lectures of Wittembach, at Basle, was a young man twenty-three years old, of small stature, of weak and sickly frame and of a temperament in which meekness and intrepidity were singularly combined. His name was LEO JUDA, the son of a priest of Alsace. He became the intimate and warmly-attached friend of Zwingle, and was his successor at Einsidlen. Leo played on the dulcimer and sang very sweetly. He studied the Oriental languages, and the works especially of Jerome and Augustus. For eighteen years at Zurich he thundered against the abominations of the papacy both from the pulpit and through the press. Assisted by others, he, at the request of his brethren, undertook the translation of the Old Testament, and toiled so severely at his task that his health gave way. When he died, one of the brightest lights of the Reformation ceased to shine in the Church below.

But among the great ones of the Reformation few were so truly great as JOHN

Calvin. Of him Theodore Beza, in whose arms he died, has left this photograph:

"Calvin was not large of stature; his complexion was pale, his eyes peculiarly bright and indicative of penetrating genius; he was equally averse to extravagance and parsimony. For many years he took but one meal a day. Of sleep he had almost none. His memory was incredible. Of the numerous details connected with the business of his office he never forgot even the most trifling, and this notwithstanding the incredible multitude of his affairs. His judgment was astonishingly acute. He despised fine speaking, and was rather abrupt in his language. He wrote admirably, and no other theologian of his time expressed himself so clearly, impressively and acutely.

"Endowed by nature with a dignified seriousness of manner and character, no one was more agreeable in ordinary conversation. He could bear in a wonderful manner with the failings of others. He never shamed any one by ill-timed reproofs, never discouraged a weak brother and never spared a willful sin. He was as powerful and strong an enemy to the vices of mankind as he was a devoted friend to truth, simplicity and uprightness. His temperament, naturally choleric, was subdued by the spirit of love.

"Having been for sixteen years a witness of his labors, I have perused the history of his life and death with all fidelity, and I now unhesitatingly testify that every Christian may find in this man the noble pattern of a truly Christian life and Christian death."

Calvin enjoyed the friendship and assistance of two excellent men, Farel and Vinet. Calvin was a deep thinker, and loved seclusion; Farel was a large-hearted, impulsive and often rash Reformer. Calvin spoke vigorously, powerfully, with abrupt energy; Vinet fascinated his hearers with the exquisite sweetness of his tone, language and manner. Luther's great theme was justification by faith; Calvin united the great idea of election with justification, and grounded the latter on the former. Luther saw in God the great Pardoner through the merits of his Son; Calvin saw God as the omnipotent, all-wise Sovereign, selecting whom he would to be the recipients of his salvation. Luther was the champion of doctrinal truth; Calvin added to his championship of the truth the rigor of the strict disciplinarian.

Calvin was born at Noyon in Picardy, July 10, 1509. His mother was a beautiful woman, his father of manly mould. Calvin enjoyed all the educational advantages of his day. He was at first destined to the priesthood, but by the advice of his father he abandoned this and became a student of law. When he was twenty years of age, his soul was suddenly aroused to a sense of sin and danger. In his trouble, finding no relief in ceremonies and masses, he flew to God in Jesus Christ, and on the death of his father, in 1523, he went to Paris, determined to become a preacher of the gospel. Now several important works issued from his mighty pen, and he was soon recognized as a leader in the great rebellion against the Roman apostasy. He prepared for Nicolas Coss, the rector of the great university of Paris, an oration full of the gospel, to be delivered on a feast-day before the people of the city. The authorities, enraged at this, attempted to arrest Coss. He escaped. They then sent officers to arrest Calvin. He escaped, being let down from the window of his bedroom in a basket.

In 1536 we find him at Geneva, where for twenty-eight years he wrought mightily in the cause of Reformation. Long before this, through the preaching of Farel and Vinet, a powerful work of reform had been accomplished in this beautiful city, and in 1535, on the 27th of August, the senate had decreed that the Reformed faith should be the religion of the State. Here Calvin became preacher and teacher of theology. After his first sermon the congregation followed him to his home to express their admiration and delight. An academy was soon organized and a catechism published. This catechism of Calvin was formally adopted by the council and citizens as containing their confession of faith. But this fervor on the part of the people gave place to indignation when, under the bold and pure teaching of the Reformer, they learned that religion, in addition to an orthodox creed, demanded a holy life, and, stung by his reproofs, they banished him from the city.

After a time, one of Calvin's leading foes in Geneva having been found guilty of crime against the State, and having perished in his attempt to escape, another having been executed for murder, and two others having fled to escape trial for treason, deputies were sent to him to entreat his return. After some natural reluctance to resume labors among so fickle a people, he re-entered Geneva in September of 1541 amid the shouts of the multitude. He addressed the crowd, reminding them of their sins and telling them, with all plainness of speech, that unless they reformed their lives he could not live among them. He preached and labored incessantly, and so great was his fame that people flocked from other countries to enjoy his preaching and instructions, whilst his judgment on ecclesiastical matters was sought for by the Reformers in every part of Europe.

Through the influence of Calvin a thorough system of ecclesiastical organization and discipline was instituted throughout the republic of Geneva—a system whose influence was powerfully felt, not only all over Protestant Switzerland, but throughout the Protestant world. According to this system, each church was organized under a body of elders, each one of equal power with all the others. This eldership formed the governing body of the particular congregation. Next above this came the provincial synod, composed, with the clergy, of elders chosen, one or two from each church, and invested with oversight and control of all the congregations within the bounds of its jurisdiction. Then over all stood the General Assembly, composed in like manner as the provincial synod, and having oversight of the whole Church.

Thus, in 1572, a powerful and flourishing Presbyterianism held the reins of influence among the snow-capped mountains of Switzerland.

GERMANY.

Memorable for ever in the history of the world will be the 10th of November, 1483, for on that day Martin Luther was born. It was the little town of Eisleben, in Saxony, that enjoyed the honor of being the birthplace of the man whose doings fill so many pages in the world's history. A solemn hour was it in the life of this man when, near to Erfurth, the thunderbolt fell at his feet, filling him with terror and teaching him a never-forgotten lesson of the power of the God he should one day serve—power to defend his friends and destroy his foes. Paul was smitten to the earth with a light above the brightness of the sun, Luther by a terrific flash of lightning. Memorable again both in his own history and in that of the world was the hour when, in the convent at Erfurth, Luther found that chained Bible that was to liberate the world!

Luther goes to Rome in behalf of seven monasteries who are quarreling with their vicar-general. On his way he tarries here and there in convents in which marble shines in walls and ornaments, silks rustle on the persons of the monks and sumptuous tables illustrate their abstemiousness. He reaches Rome. He enters the northern gate, and falling on his knees, exclaims, "Holy Rome, I salute thee!" Amazed and horror-stricken at the pride, luxury, licentiousness and profanity of all classes in Rome, he goes to the Santa Scala, that staircase of Pilate brought miraculously to Rome, and on his knees he creeps up, saying his *aves* and *credos*, when suddenly a voice of thunder in his heart cries out, "The just shall live by faith!" He hastens from

Rome, and now at length, in 1517, we see him, a full-grown man, standing before the door of the church of All Saints in Wittenberg. There he stands, his eyes full of fire, a stern, solemn countenance, brave, high spirited, intrepid, a hammer in one hand, a paper in the other. It is the 31st of October, at noon, on the day before the festival of All Saints. The church had been built by the elector and was full of relics. On its door he nails the paper containing the ninety-five theses.

It was the shameless conduct of the shameless Tetzel that spurred Luther to this daring defiance of Rome. This man, a notorious adulterer, had come to Wittenberg to revive the traffic in indulgences. Pope Leo X. needed money, and Tetzel was gathering it for him. This traffic in indulgences had ever been a fertile source of replenishment to the papal exchequer. Tetzel boasted that he had saved more souls by indulgences than St. Peter ever saved by his preaching. "I was compelled in my conscience," wrote Luther, "to expose the scandalous sale of indulgences. I found myself in it alone, and as it were by surprise; and when it became impossible for me to retreat, I made many concessions to the pope, not, however, in many important points, but certainly at the time I adored him in earnest."

This act of Luther amazed Europe and won applause from thousands who, while they admired, lacked the courage to imitate his heroism, for it was a fearful thing to lift the hand against the power that had come to overshadow the civilized world. At first, indeed, Pope Leo smiled at the opposition of this monk as a giant would smile at the resistance of a little child. But before a year had gone by his Holiness began to perceive that the Reformer was more than a child, and he issued his mandate bidding Luther within sixty days to present himself before the inquisitor-general at Rome. Frederick, elector of Saxony, Luther's friend, obtained leave for the trial of Luther in Germany before Cardinal Cajetan. But, sixteen days after the citation to the bar of Cajetan, the bishop of Acoli, auditor of the apostolic chamber at Rome, condemned Luther as an incorrigible heretic. Luther presented himself at the bar of Cajetan, at Augsburg, but finding no prospect of a fair hearing, he withdrew to Wittenberg and appealed from the pope ill informed to the pope better informed.

The ripeness of Europe for reform is abundantly evident from the marvelous impression produced by the stand taken by Luther, and the wonderful esteem in which his name was held not only notwithstanding, but because of his opposition to the pope. Charles Miltitz, a Saxon knight, being sent, in 1519, to negotiate with Luther in the name of the pope, said, "Martin, you have united the whole world to you and drawn it from the pope. I have discovered this at the inns on my way from Rome to Wittenberg. You are so much favored with the popular opinion that I could not with the help of twenty-five hundred soldiers compel you to follow me to Rome."

Toward the close of this year, Luther with new light in his heart, began to proclaim that in the sacrament of the Lord's Supper both bread and wine ought to be administered to the communicants. This called down another storm of indignation from the bond-slaves of the papacy.

In June, 1520, forty-one propositions from Luther's works, which in the shape of tracts, sermons, commentaries and letters now flooded Europe, were condemned as heretical, the reading of his works forbidden on pain of excommunication, whilst such as had copies in their possession were commanded to burn them, and Luther himself was charged within sixty days to recant under pain of excommunication and final deliverance to Satan. Luther, fearless alike of Satan and the pope, raised a great pile of wood outside the walls of Wittenberg, and there, in the presence of the professors and students of the university and of the vast crowd of citizens, committed to the flames the papal bull, together with the volumes of the canon law, the rule of the papal jurisdiction, and thus for ever separated himself from the Church of Rome!

Free now from all obligations to his old master, Luther set himself thoroughly to reform the worship and doctrine of the church at Wittenberg, and of all the churches where his influence prevailed. In this work of God he was warmly and efficiently aided by large numbers of the learned in various parts of Europe. So rapidly spread the work, and so formidable were the proportions it assumed, that some extraordinary measures had become necessary to prevent the overthrow of the papacy in large portions of the German empire. Accordingly, the emperor convened at Worms the General Assembly of the empire, composed of its princes, archbishops, bishops and many of its abbots. No sooner was the body well organized than the legate of the pope demanded the condemnation of Luther. But Luther's friends were too many and too wise to consent to procedure against the Reformer in his absence, and without opportunity to answer for himself at the imperial tribunal. At the appearance at Worms of the man to whom God had granted the power and privilege of wielding the truth so mightily vast crowds came together, and even those who dreaded or hated his doctrine were filled with admiration at his intrepidity. For two hours, first in German, then in Latin, he expounded and defended the truth as he understood it, winning applause from a large proportion of the assembly. But, lo! a sudden command from the emperor dismissed him to his home, after which the diet declared him an excommunicated heretic! To prevent his assassination, his good friend, the elector Frederic, sent horsemen to waylay him and hurry him to the castle of Wartburg, where for ten months he lay concealed from the knowledge and power of his enemies.

In March, 1522, he reappeared at Wittenberg, and soon issued his translations of the New Testament. Copies of it were multiplied and circulated. It was read by all classes with amazing avidity, and wherever read it was to the church of Rome like a light kindled in a chamber long closed, revealing dust and spiders and bats' nests and all manner of abominations.

In 1525, Luther lost his efficient patron, Frederick the Wise, who was, however, succeeded by his brother John, both in the electorship and in the patronship of the Reformation. John at once took a decided stand. He placed himself at the head of the Reformers, provided a new order of worship, placed well-qualified pastors over the congregations, ordered the sacramental services to be administered in the German tongue and sent heralds through the empire to proclaim these important regulations. Stimulated by this bold and heroic conduct, other princes and other states joined in the work of reform, and accepted and proclaimed a similar form of worship, doctrine and discipline. From every part of Germany now came the call for men to preach a gospel faith in the ears of a waiting, eager people.

On the left bank of the Rhine, forty miles north of Mayence, is the ancient town of Speyer or Spires. It has walls and ditches and five gates, and a venerable old cathedral that once contained the ashes of eight emperors, three empresses and two imperial princesses.

In this town two very important imperial diets were held. The first assembled in 1526, and at this an attempt was made, though successfully resisted, to decree an enforcement of the condemnation passed against Luther and his adherents at the diet of Worms. The emperor was requested instead to call a full ecclesiastical council for the final adjustment of difficulties, and in the mean time each state and prince was left to its own discretion in matters pertaining to religion. Free for the time from persecuting hindrance, the precious leaven spread through the meal, and Luther put forth all his strength to consolidate the acquisitions thus far won to the cause of right and truth.

But in 1529, much sooner than was anticipated, Charles V. convoked the second imperial diet at Spires, which annulled the provisions of its predecessor three years before, and declared every change in doctrine, discipline and worship unlawful until the decision of a general council could be had. Against this decision, as iniquitous and intolerable, the elector of Saxony, the marquis of Brandenburg, the landgrave of Hesse, the dukes of Lunenburg, the prince of Anhalt, with the deputies of fourteen imperial cities, on the 19th of April, solemnly PROTESTED. Thus arose the term PROTESTANTS.

The next year the diet was held at Augsburg, a city of Bavaria, thirty-five miles north-west of Munich. It is a fine old town. A group of government offices is now covered by what was the roof of the episcopal palace beneath which the "Confession of Augsburg" was presented to the emperor Charles V. To the diet at this place Charles had come in June, 1530, determined to effect some adjustment of the ecclesiastical troubles of the empire. Luther was ordered to present a scheme embracing the chief points of religious doctrine. He accordingly presented seventeen articles of faith agreed upon at Torgau. These were enlarged by Melanchthon at the request of the princes, and the result of his work forms the noted "Augsburg Confession." It contained twenty-eight chapters, and was publicly read in the diet. But the diet passed decrees against the Reformers more violent even than those of Worms. Nothing daunted, Luther exhorted the Protestant princes to courage and firmness. They met later in the year at Schmalkalden, and formed a league of defence against all aggressors, applying to France, England and Denmark for aid. Through their favor the Protestant princes, in 1532, secured a treaty with Charles at Nuremberg which amounted almost to a free toleration of

Protestantism. Now again the Reformers throughout Europe, thanking God, took fresh courage and pushed on the work of God. This same year Henry VIII. was divorced from Queen Catharine and married to Anne Boleyn.

A vast body of Protestants now lay in the heart of Germany, and for twelve or fifteen years, by dint of courage and vigilance, they not only held their ground, but extended their conquests. Rome became furious, and in 1541 gathered her adherents in conclave at Trent among the Tyrolese mountains. This council embraced six cardinals, thirty-two archbishops, two hundred and twenty-eight bishops and a multitude of inferior clergy. The Protestant princes met in diet at Ratisbon, and protested against the authority of the conclave at Trent. The emperor took up arms against the princes, and defeated them in a bloody battle. And now followed years of struggle, distress, humiliation for the Reformers and their followers, yet in many a province and city of growth in knowledge, purity and strength.

During the years that followed the nailing of the theses to the door of All Saints church at Wittenberg, city after city and province after province had joined the cause of reform. At the head of the procession of cities came *Magdeburg*. There Luther had gone to school, and many of his old acquaintances and personal friends were in authority and influence. One day an old weaver was arrested for singing a Lutheran hymn and offering it for sale. The citizens rose, met in a churchyard and appointed a committee of eight to manage church matters and appoint preachers. Other parishes followed the example. At length, on the 17th of June, 1524, the sacrament of the Supper was administered after the Lutheran manner in all the churches of the old town.

At *Brunswick*, and in most of the towns in this part of Germany, things took very much the same course. In all of them preachers of the truth appear, Lutheran hymns are sung by the people and the town council first resists and then gives way. In *Goelar* fifty men were appointed from the various parishes to carry out the plans of Reform. At *Göttingen* the people compelled the overseers of the commune to acquiesce in their schemes. At *Eimbeck* the commune compelled the council to recall the preacher they had dismissed at the request of the canons. In *Bremen* the pulpits had become Lutheran as early as 1525. In *Lubeck*, where the patrician families were in close alliance with the clergy, Luther's commentary on the Scriptures was burned in the market-place. The citizens rose and appointed a committee of sixty-four to manage the Reform. They recalled the expelled preachers, removed the adherents of Rome from every pulpit in the city and converted convents into schools and hospitals.

"So powerfully did the spirit of the Reformation diffuse itself through Lower Germany. Already it had taken possession of a portion of the principalities; it was triumphant in the Wendish cities; it had penetrated into Westphalia, and seemed about to pervade the whole character and condition of Northern Germany." In April, 1535, the preachers of Bremen, Hamburg, Lubeck, Rostock, Stralsund and Lüneburg entered into a convention in which they determined that in future no one should be permitted to preach who did not solemnly subscribe to the Augsburg Confession.

Thus the great conflict went on. At length, Maurice, now elector of Saxony, after years of skillful management, suddenly flew to arms in the Protestant cause. Attacking the emperor, he came near capturing him at Innspruck, in 1552. Just at this time also Henry II. of France declared war against Charles, and the latter, yielding to necessity, opened negotiations with the Protestant princes assembled at Passau. The treaty of Passau guaranteed to the Protestants the free exercise of their religion, and pledged a diet of the empire for the settlement of the great religious question upon a reasonable and firm foundation. The diet met at Augsburg in 1555, and there finally concluded the celebrated "Peace of Religion," which gave religious freedom to Germany and established the Reformation.

In this settlement it was agreed "that the Protestants who followed the Confession of Augsburg should be for the future considered as entirely exempt from the jurisdiction of the Roman pontiff, and from the authority and superintendence of the bishops; that they were left at perfect liberty to enact laws for themselves relating to their religious sentiments, discipline and worship; that all the inhabitants of the German empire should be allowed to judge for themselves in questions relating to religious matters and to join themselves to that Church whose doctrine and worship they thought the purest and the most consonant to the spirit of Christianity; and that all those who should injure or persecute any person under religious pretexts and on account of their opinions should be declared and proceeded against as public enemies of the empire, invaders of its liberty and disturbers of its peace."

Of such immeasurable importance and imposing grandeur was the work achieved by the blessing of God through the piety, learning and heroism of Luther and his coadjutors during the period of thirty-eight years between the years 1517, when the theses were nailed to the door of the church of All Saints at Wittenberg, and the year 1555, when the diet of Augsburg decreed this religious settlement.

Such, in the main, was the condition of religious affairs in Germany in 1572, just about one half century after the birth of the Reformation. The Church was for the most part at peace, whilst Luther and Melanchthon were sleeping side by side in the church of All Saints at Wittenberg.

FRANCE.

Turn we now to beautiful, guilty France. To France, God, in his providence, proffered the office and glory of being the banner-bearer to the Reformation. While Luther, in 1517, was climbing the Santa Scala at Rome on his knees and mumbling his *Ave Marias,* while Zwingle was fighting as a soldier in the pope's Swiss army, a great, deep work of grace was going on in France. Before this time the aged Lefèvre had exclaimed to his youthful pupil, Farel, "My dear William, God will change the face of the world, and you will see it!" Before this, Lefèvre, turning with disgust from a compilation of the lives of the saints, which he said were fit only as "brimstone to kindle the fires of idolatry," completed his commentaries on the Epistles of St. Paul. Before this he had discovered and proclaimed in the Sorbonne itself, "It is God alone who by his grace justifies unto eternal life. There is a righteousness of our own works, and a righteousness which is of grace; the one of man, the other of God; the one earthy and passing away, the other divine and everlasting; the one discovering sin and bringing the fear of death, the other revealing grace for the attainment of life."

To these truths Farel and crowds of others listened with delight, and some noble spirits even now embraced the truth, and girding on their armor, enlisted for the war.

"Thus, if we regard dates," writes D'Aubigné, "we must confess that neither to Switzerland nor to Germany belongs the honor of having been first in the work. That honor belongs to France. It was Lefèvre and Farel who were first awakened by the voice of that trumpet which sounded from heaven in the sixteenth century, and who were earliest in the field on foot and under arms."

Meanwhile there were two young people growing up together in the French court who were to exert no small influence on the cause. One was a prince, tall and of striking features and a slave to his passions; the other was his sister, vigorous in understanding and of fine talents, natural and acquired. The one, in 1515, became Francis I., king of France, the other was the princess Margaret of Valois, whom the king loved with exceeding tenderness. Margaret was of fine person, passionately fond of literature and full of wit. Her masculine judgment was often of great service to the king, her brother, in matters of moment to the State. Surrounded by the most disgusting licentiousness, she turned from the world to the gospel. She listened to Lefèvre, to Farel, to Briçonnet, the bishop of Meaux, and became a follower of Christ. "Thus, in the glittering court of Francis I., and in the dissolute house of Louise of Savoy, was wrought one of those conversions which in every age are the work of the word of God."

Had Francis but followed in the steps of his beautiful and accomplished sister! But this was not to be. His mother and Margaret's, Louise of Savoy, infamous for iniquities, was more powerful with her son than was the word of God. Her every wicked wish was seconded and executed by her favorite, Duprat, "the most vicious of bipeds." With them soon went the Sorbonne, followed by the whole rabble of ignorant priests, into furious opposition to the nascent Reformation.

But the word of God grew—grew mightily. There was at court a gentleman of Artois, named Louis Berquin. Pure in life, of extensive and accurate knowledge, he was also distinguished for the fervor of his attachment to his friends and for his compassion for the poor. He had a perfect horror of all dissimulation, and could not endure the sight of oppression. Opposition to him on the part of the wicked drove him to the Bible; it led him to Christ, and from this time Margaret, Briçonnet and Lefèvre had a coadjutor in Louis Berquin.

The work spread with wonderful rapidity. In no other country in Europe did the Reformation meet with a reception so prompt, so warm, so general. "The danger," said the foe, "is every day greater; already the heretical sentiments are counted as those of the best-informed classes; the devouring flame is circulating between the rafters; the conflagration will presently burst forth, and the structure of the established faith will fall with sudden crash to the earth."

Persecuted in Paris, the Reformation spread into the provinces; Farel, Mosurier, Gerold Roussel and his brother Arnaud left Paris and were warmly welcomed by Briçonnet at Meaux. There, in his own diocese, this man toiled unceasingly. He visited all the parishes, called together all the clergy and all the church officers, catechised them, lectured them, exhorted them. In 1519 he summoned a synod of all the clergy in his diocese, and having examined one hundred and twenty-seven, found only fourteen of whom he could approve.

In 1524, Lefèvre published a French translation of the New Testament, and the next year a like version of the Psalms.

Copies of the precious volume were multiplied. They passed from hand to hand. They were read in the family and in the closet, and thus many new recruits were enrolled in the army of the Reformation. In the city of Meaux "many were taken with so ardent a desire to know the way of salvation that artisans, carders, fullers and combers, while at work with their hands, had their thoughts engaged on the word of God. On Sundays and on festivals they employed themselves in reading the Scriptures and in inquiring into the good pleasure of the Lord."

Through Margaret portions of the French version of the Scriptures were presented to her brother and mother. Nothing is impossible with God. Even Louise of Savoy might be converted!

At Meaux the word reached John Leclerc, a wool-carder. He was a man of martyr courage, full of zeal, and a natural leader of men in dangerous times. He went from house to house, strengthening and confirming the disciples in their faith. He wrote a proclamation against the Roman antichrist in which he declared that God would overthrow the monster, and he nailed his proclamation to the door of the cathedral. Rome, stung to madness, threw the offender into prison, whipped him through the streets three days in succession, his blood marking his progress, and then on the third day branded him on the forehead with a hot iron. His mother looked on with all a mother's anguish, and then shrieked out, "Glory be to Jesus Christ and his witnesses!" The scarred confessor withdrew to Metz, where, for breaking the graven images which the people worshiped, he was burned alive at a slow fire, and thus died, the first of a long, awfully long, list of martyrs to the gospel in France.

But Metz had been occupied with the truth. Through the labors of Leclerc, John Châtelain and Peter Toussaint the word found its way into many families, and among them not a few of high degree.

The persecutions that drove the saints from Paris and Meaux only scattered the seed. The exiles went everywhere, preaching the word, and great results began to show themselves in the countries of the Saône, the Rhone and the Alps. Anemond, a knight of Dauphiny, entered the ranks of the gospel. Active, ardent, ever impetuous, his zeal gave him no rest. Full of enthusiasm, he went to Switzerland and then to Wittenberg, and did his utmost to persuade Luther and Zwingle to go with him to France, for he was sure they could carry all before them.

Francis I., accompanied by his sister Margaret, led an army through Lyons to battle with the soldiers of Charles V. In company with Margaret was her Christian almoner, Michel d'Arande. At the command of Margaret, Michel boldly proclaimed the pure gospel to a great company drawn together by the novelty of the occasion, by desire to hear the word and by the favor with which the preacher and his doctrine were regarded by the sister of the king. Co-operating with Michel was another man of great piety and discretion, Anthony Papillon, an accomplished scholar and, through the influence of Margaret, an incumbent in office under the king and member of the council. Thus Lyons became a centre of truth from which the rays shot abroad far and wide into the surrounding darkness. Michel d'Arande, under the protection of Margaret, kindled the gospel fires in Maçon. Papillon and Du Blet sounded the trumpet in Grenoble. As early as 1524 there existed in Basle a Bible society, a religious tract society and an association of colporteurs whose chief efforts were directed to the work of evangelization in France. The agents of these societies, poor, pious men, went here and there, from house to house, knocking at every door and offering to all the bread of life.

Thus, amid hindrances and oppositions, the work of Christ in France went grandly on. In this city, in that village, in this and that lone hamlet, Christ crucified became known and embraced, and souls were saved and God was glorified.

In 1535 the Psalms of David were translated, versified and set to melodious music, and French fervor, vivacity and enthusiasm, under the impulse of evangelical spirit, poured itself forth in sacred song. "This holy ordinance charmed the ears, hearts and affections of court and city, town and country." These sacred songs "were sung in the Louvre as well as in the Pres des Clercs by ladies, princes and by Henry II. himself. This one ordinance alone contributed mightily to the downfall of popery and the propagation of the gospel. It accorded so well with the genius of the nation that all ranks and degrees of men practiced it in the temples and in their families. No gentleman professing the Reformed religion would sit down at his table without praising God by singing."

On went the glorious work. Churches were gathered and duly organized. Consultations were held. Creeds and confessions were compiled. In 1559, just one year before the first General Assembly of the Church of Scotland, the first General Assembly of the French Protestant Church was held in Paris. This assembly drew up a confession of faith and canons of discipline. In this work the state had no hand. It was wholly the work of the Church herself; and though an independent work, an original embodiment of principles of doctrine fresh from the word of God, "it was remarkably harmonious with the confessions of other Protestant Churches, showing that under the teaching of God's spirit no good men, wherever they may be scattered and whatever their circumstances of trial, seriously differ in their interpretations of Scripture." In 1561, Beza presented a copy of this formulary to Charles IX. in the colloquy at Poissy. It was confirmed in the national council of Rochelle, and signed by Condé, Nassau, Coligny and the synod, by the queen of Navarre, and her son, Henry

IV., and was recognized by the Reformed of the French nation.

In this confession and canons we read, "That the church in whose service a minister dieth shall take care of his widow and orphans; and if the church cannot do it through want of ability, the province shall maintain them."

"The churches shall do their utmost endeavor to erect schools and take care of the instruction of their youth, and all ministers shall endeavor to catechise every one of their flocks once or twice a year, and shall exhort them to conform themselves thereunto very carefully."

"Every church shall endeavor to maintain its own poor."

"Fathers and mothers shall be exhorted to be very careful of their children's education, which are the seed-plot and promising hopes of God's Church. And, therefore, such as send them to school to be taught by priests, monks, Jesuits and nuns, they shall be prosecuted with all church censures."

Concerning the state of the French Protestant Church at this time a contemporary writer says: "The holy word of God is truly, duly and powerfully preached in churches and fields, in ships and houses, in vaults and cellars, in all places where gospel ministers can have admission and conveniency, and with singular success. Multitudes are convinced and converted, established and edified. Christ rideth out upon the white horse of the ministry with the sword and bow of the gospel preacher, conquering and to conquer. Multitudes flock in like doves into the windows of God. As innumerable drops of dew fall from the womb of the morning, so hath the Lord Christ the dew of his youth. The popish churches are drained, the Protestant temples are filled. The priests complain that their altars are neglected; their masses are now indeed solitary. Dagon cannot stand before God's ark."

During the twelve years that followed the meeting of the first General Assembly in Paris there was a grand advance of the Christian army. In the year preceding the awful 1572 the French General Assembly met at Rochelle. In this assembly Theodore Beza presided as moderator, and there were present the queen of Navarre, the prince of Navarre, Henry de Bourbon, prince of Condé, Prince Lewis, count of Nassau, the admiral Coligny and other lords and gentlemen. That General Assembly represented and ruled over twenty-one hundred and fifty churches. In some of these churches there were ten thousand members. The church of Orleans had seven thousand communicants and five ministers. In the province of Normandy there were three hundred and five pastors, and sixty in Provence.

Such was the Presbyterianism of France at the opening of the year of massacre, 1572.

THE NETHERLANDS.

Where people are free they will think, and where people think popery is always in peril, for under the shadows of well-organized popery the thinking is mostly done by proxy. What timid, sluggish thinking is done by the people must pass along the grooves channeled for them by an infallible pope and the subordinates taught and coerced by him. If an Abbé Michaud or a Döllinger dare to think outside of these grooves, he is smitten with the bolts of excommunication, and the poor Marets and Gratrys and Hefeles and Spauldings and Kenricks, who to-day think the truth, to-morrow, when the pope speaks, go down on their knees, beg pardon and pledge themselves henceforth to think not their own but the pope's thoughts.

The Netherlanders were largely a free people. They were, therefore, a thinking people. They were a commercial and industrious people, and hence they made very poor Romish slaves. For the life of them they could not see why the masses should toil and scheme and pay taxes and fight in the armies, while thousands of idle nuns and gross, fat monks should live in idleness, "trade in indulgences, squander in taverns" and revel in all sorts of licentiousness. Hence, writes Motley, "it was impossible that they, the most energetic and quick-witted people in Europe, should not feel sympathy with the great effort made by Christendom to shake off the incubus that had so long paralyzed her hands and brain."

"At the era of the Reformation," writes D'Aubigné, "the Netherlands was one of the most flourishing countries of Europe. Situated at the very gates of Germany, it would be one of the first to hear the report of the Reformation. Two very distinct parties composed its population. The more southern, that overflowed with wealth, gave way. How could all these manufactories, carried to the highest degree of perfection, this immense commerce by land and sea, Bruges, the great mart of the northern trade, Antwerp, the queen of the merchant cities,—how could all these resign themselves to a long and bloody struggle about questions of faith? On the contrary, the northern provinces, defended by their sand-hills, the sea and their canals, and still more by their simplicity of manners and their determination to lose everything rather than the gospel, not only preserved their freedom, their privileges and their faith, but even achieved their independence and a glorious nationality." Few spots on this planet of ours have become the monuments of grander heroism in assault, defence and endurance than that narrow, half-drowned triangle shut in between France, Germany and the sea.

From the earliest times the Netherlands had shown the spirit of revolt from the tyrannies and sins of Rome. By the middle of the twelfth century the gospel heresy had there become troublesome to his Holiness. Then came the Waldenses, Albigenses, Lollards, Bohemian Brothers, to war in the Netherlands the war of faith and suffering, and there to endure the martyr's death. Not even in Spain or Italy did ingenuity ever devise forms of saint-murder more horrid than issued from the fertile wickedness of the monks in the Netherlands. In Flanders the heretic was stripped, bound to the stake, flayed from the neck to the navel, and swarms of bees let loose upon him to torture him to death. The curse pronounced upon the poor sufferers was truly Roman. The curser stood with a waxen torch in each hand, and in these words he cursed: "In the name of the Father, the Son and the Holy Ghost, the blessed Virgin Mary, John the Baptist, Peter and Paul, and all other saints in heaven, we do curse and cut off from our communion him who has thus rebelled against us. May the curse strike him in his house, barn, bed, field, path, city and castle! May he be cursed in battle, in praying, in speaking, in silence, in eating, in drinking, in sleeping! May he be accursed in his taste, hearing, smelling and in all his senses! May the curse blast his eyes, his head and his body, from his crown to the soles of his feet! I conjure you, devil and all your imps, that you take no rest till you have brought him to eternal shame. I command you, devil and all your imps, that even as I now blow out these torches you do immediately extinguish the light from his eyes. So be it, so be it! Amen and amen!" And then the gentle soul blew out the torches!

But still the good work went on. The Bible, translated by Waldo into French, and rendered into Netherland verse, added to the number of converts. Toward the end of the fourteenth century the gales of heaven bore the doctrines of Wickliffe over the land. Erasmus did good service in exposing the abominations of popery. Imperial edicts sought to resist the tide. One of them, in 1521, assured the people that "Martin Luther was a devil in human form, clothed in the dress of a priest." In

1523 a Dutch translation of the New Testament was published and circulated, whilst two Christians were burned at Brussels, and the martyrdoms and the Bible alike made new converts. Crowds of believers, driven from the city of Antwerp, assembled on the banks of the Scheldt to listen to the word of life. In 1536, William Tyndale, the translator of the New Testament for England, arrested at Antwerp, was brought to the stake near Brussels, and first strangled and then burned, crying with his last words, "Lord, open the eyes of the king of England!" Other witnesses followed through bold service to the martyr's grave.

In 1555, Charles V., now fifty-five years of age, abdicated in favor of his son, Philip II., bequeathing to the Netherlands the Spanish Inquisition, more than fifty thousand martyrs' graves and a war of eighty years that swallowed up millions more of human lives, together with an edict (which was re-enacted by his successor) to the following effect:

"No one shall print, write, copy, keep, conceal, sell, buy or give in the churches, streets or other places any book or writing made by Martin Luther, John Œcolampadius, Ulrich Zwinglius, Martin Bucer, John Calvin or other heretics reprobated by the Holy Church, nor break or otherwise injure the image of the holy Virgin or canonized saints, nor in his house hold conventicles or illegal gatherings, or be present at any time in which the adherents of the above-mentioned heretics teach, baptize and form conspiracies against the holy Church and the general welfare.

"Moreover, we forbid all persons to *converse or dispute concerning the holy Scriptures*, openly or secretly, especially upon any doubtful or difficult matters, or *to read, teach or expound the Scriptures*, unless they have studied theology and been approved by some renowned university, or to preach secretly or openly, or *to entertain any of the opinions* of the above-named heretics."

All who violate this edict are to be punished as follows, to wit: "The men with the sword and the women to be buried alive, if they *do not persist* in their errors; if they *do* persist in them, they are to be executed with fire; all their property, in both cases, being confiscated to the crown." And, further, any persons who "lodge, entertain, furnish with food, fire or clothing, or otherwise favor any one holden or notoriously suspected of being a heretic, or failing to denounce any such persons, shall be liable to the above-mentioned punishments."

In 1559, Philip II. withdrew to Spain, never to return to the Netherlands, leaving behind as regent the base-born Margaret of Parma. The next year the pope and Philip appointed three archbishoprics and fifteen bishoprics, whose incumbents were to work the inquisitorial machine.

The appointment of these officers aroused a powerful opposition, drew attention more than ever to the doctrines of the Reformers and greatly increased the number of professed Protestants. Tracts were everywhere

PHILIP II.

Page 98.

distributed and largely read. Preachers boldly proclaimed the truth. The people assembled by thousands and went in procession to the churches, chanting the psalms of David.

But the enemy was not idle. In 1564 the pastor of the Reformed church at Antwerp was seized, and having been tortured by the Inquisition, was led out to execution. A vast crowd surged around the place of burning, and just as they were making an onset for the rescue of the confessor the executioner made his work sure by stabbing his victim to the heart!

As the Reformers were forbidden to assemble in chapels, in 1566 they inaugurated a new era in the Reformation by adopting the system of worshiping in the open fields. Forth from the city gates they streamed in vast processions, and there, under the open sky, worshiped the God of heaven. This custom began in West Flanders, passed thence into Brabant, and then spread with such rapidity into the other provinces that soon there was not a lowland city but had its meeting, attended sometimes even by tens of thousands. The preachers exhibited heroic courage and amazing zeal. Many of the Reformed clergy were men of ripe scholarship, graceful accomplishments and fervid eloquence. Among them was Peregrinne de la Grange, of noble blood and of fiery spirit, "who galloped to the field, preached on horseback, and fired a pistol as a signal for the congregation to give attention." On Sundays and holidays there was preaching in the vicinity of the large towns; and as the people were sometimes assailed during the time of worship, they at length found it needful to furnish themselves with weapons of defence. When they assembled, they placed the women and children around the pulpit; next around them the men congregated, and beyond the circle of worshipers a patrol was stationed. Sometimes for four hours together they listened, prayed and sung. When the service was over, the crowd escorted their preacher to the town and furnished him with hospitable entertainment.

And now the time for something like formal organization had come. As yet there was no common bond among the Protestants of the Netherlands, except that which united them in faith to their common Lord. In 1562, however, the Netherland Christians drew up a treatise under the title of "A Confession of Faith generally maintained by believers dispersed throughout the Low Countries, who desire to live according to the purity of the holy gospel of our Lord Jesus Christ." It was sent to Geneva to be revised by Calvin, and having received his approval, was printed in Dutch and German.

Thus the year 1572 found a powerful Presbyterian church in the Netherlands, baptized in blood and flame as perhaps was no other church, excepting that of the Waldenses. The northern provinces, Holland, Zealand, Utrecht and Friesland, were almost unanimous in the faith, and large numbers of like belief were scattered throughout the southern portion of the land.

ENGLAND.

If to the Italians in the strongholds of the Piedmontese valleys it was given to continue the evangelical succession from the times of the apostles, the honor of sounding the first bugle-blast of Reform and of rebellion against Rome was conferred upon an Englishman. "If Luther and Calvin are the fathers of the Reformation, Wickliffe is its grandfather." His translation of the New Testament into English not only showed the true path to reform, but sowed the fair fields of England with the seeds of life for coming generations. Grass-blades of living green shot up in many a favored spot. Parliament was petitioned for Reform. Wickliffian theses, the "Twelve Conclusions," were fixed to the gates of St. Paul's and Westminster Abbey. William Sautre, for saying, "Instead of adoring the cross on which Christ suffered, I adore Christ who suffered on it," became the proto-martyr of Protestantism. In March, 1401, more than eighty years before Luther was born, Santre was burned alive at Smithfield. That Lollard tower, opposite the new Parliament house on the Thames embankment, was filled with victims. Sixteen years after this the brave old Lord Cobham, for the sin of confessing Christ, was dragged on a hurdle to St. Giles' Fields, and there, suspended by chains over a slow fire, he was burned to death.

But the smoke of martyrdom infected all it blew upon. The ashes of the martyr-fires scattered through the kingdom broke out not in "blains upon man and beast," but in deep, exciting thought, in great questionings of heart, in anxious perusal of the holy word, in prayer and in numerous conversions. The leaven crept through the masses from mind to mind, from heart to heart; and ere King Henry had thought of his divorce the divine Husbandman had crops ripening all over the kingdom.

Thus the work in England was not the work of the many-wived Henry, nor was it largely the work of great men. "Those mighty personages we meet with in Germany, Switzerland and France—men like Luther, Zwingle and Calvin—do not appear in England, but the holy Scripture is widely circulated."

About the time that Luther fixed his theses to the door of All Saints, Wittenberg, the New Testament in the Greek and Latin came to England from the press of Basle, and produced an amazing sensation. "It was in every hand; men struggled to procure it, read it eagerly, and would even kiss it." Never was there such a searching of the sacred word. The result was Protestantism.

Take one example in a thousand. In Trinity college, Cambridge, there is a keen-witted but modest, even bashful young man. Troubled in soul, he applies to his priest for advice. The priest prescribes vigils and fastings. The sufferer suffers all the more. His soul cannot feed itself on husks. He hears of a wonderful book. Obtaining a copy, he reads and is amazed. At length he comes upon the words, "This is a faithful saying, and worthy of all acceptation, that Christ Jesus came into the world to save sinners, of whom I am chief." "Ah!" he exclaims, "at last I have heard of Jesus! My vigils and fastings and pilgrimages and masses were slaying me. Jesus saves." This was Thomas Bilney. He was arrested, but on the fourth appearance before his judges his courage failed, and he recanted and went back to freedom and misery. But he revived, and now he went about preaching the truth in private houses, in open fields, bewailing his weakness and his sin. Again he was arrested, and in 1531 he was made the victim of that truly Roman Catholic remedy for opposition to its corruptions, burning to death at the stake.

But still the wind blew the smoke and

ashes of martyrdom abroad, infecting other hundreds and thousands. England is pervaded, and is all alive with the holy leaven.

And now a new seed-sower came. William Tyndale had translated the New Testament into English. It had been printed partly at Cologne, partly at Worms. In 1525 it was brought stealthily across the sea and up the Thames and by night to Honey lane, a narrow thoroughfare adjoining Cheapside, to the house of a poor and pious curate, Thomas Garret. He read until at last he sighed, "His word was in mine heart as a burning fire shut up in my bones, and I was weary with forbearing and I could not stay." So he went abroad with the word. He sold it to laymen and priests and monks, and thus the word went unbound through the realm.

The blessed word was read with amazing avidity and delight. Women committed the Gospels and Epistles to memory. One woman gave a copy of the Epistles of Paul to her son, saying, "My son, live according to these writing, and not according to the teachings of the clergy." He read three Epistles. He procured the whole New Testament, and read it through many times. One day, learning that Bilney was preaching at Ipswich, he went to hear him, and exclaimed, "Oh what a sermon! How full of the Holy Ghost!"

Now meetings for reading and hearing the word and for prayer began to be multiplied. Not only the cottages of the poor, but in some instances the palaces of the rich, were opened for these meetings. Among these was Bower Hall, the residence of the squires of Bumpstead, and Foxe and Topley and Tyball often read the Scriptures there in the presence of the master and all his household.

Rome says that we can know the Scriptures only through the Romish Church. How, then, did the cottagers of England so quickly recognize the word of God? I have a father, suppose, whom I have never seen, but I have heard of him; I know much about him, and now letter after letter purporting to come from him is put into my hand. I read, and I know that no one but my own dear father could write thus to me. So the human spirit, under the tuition of the Holy Spirit, knows that the pages of the Bible are alive with the words and thoughts of the great, good Father in heaven.

But while the word of God is thus making its way among the *people* of England, Wolsey has fallen, the king is divorced and Henry VIII. is become a pope in England. And now began a fearful struggle between the new pope and his Christian subjects. They had learned the will of God from God's own book, and they must accept it as the rule of duty, King Henry's will! From that day to this the headship of the monarch in the English Church has been the source of nearly all its weakness and of its many and fearful corruptions.

In 1539 the king appointed a commission to draw up articles for the direction of the Church in doctrine and worship.

Six articles were the result, enjoining upon the whole realm, on penalty of imprisonment, forfeiture of property, or death as heretics, these items: The real presence in the sacrament, communion in one kind only, the celibacy of the priesthood, the strict observance of vows of chastity, priests' masses and auricular confession. Thus the government would compel the retention of a meagrely modified popery, while the seeds of a pure religion were bearing rich and ample fruit among the masses. In the collision between these two forces multitudes of God's own people were ground to powder.

The question is not without interest, though it is more easily asked than answered, How early in England did *a distinctive Presbyterianism* make its appearance? On the Continent, under the lead of highly gifted men interpreting to the people the word of God, the Church in abandoning the papacy unanimously betook itself to Presbyterianism. It would be very strange, therefore, if in England, where the real Reformation originated among the people, under the teachings of the New Testament, the same form of Church polity should not have asserted and made good its claims. Harassed by persecution, there was for some time little thought except how to feed the soul with the food of salvation. But even in their earlier efforts to live they found that preachers were a necessity, and that in pressing exigencies the Church, the little assembly of hated, hunted believers, were fully competent to appoint a ministry without leave of priest, bishop or pope. This right carried with it the right to model the worship of Christian assemblies in accordance with their view of the teachings of God's word, the mandate of a more than semi-popish sovereign to the contrary notwithstanding. From the collision between this humble Church and the government sprang Puritanism. This Puritanism was partly Episcopal, more largely independent, very largely Presbyterian.

Perhaps the earliest formal Presbyterianism in the realm was foreign rather than native.

In the English Channel, one hundred and sixty miles south-west of Southampton, is the triangular, rock-girt island of Guernsey, having in our day a population of thirty thousand. In the tenth century it bore the name of the Holy Isle, on account of the swarms of monks and ecclesiastics that infested it. South-east of Guernsey is the quadrangular isle of Jersey, with its high northern coast, from which its surface slopes along toward the south. It has now a population of nearly sixty thousand souls.

These islands, so near the coast of France, offered a tempting asylum to the hunted Huguenots, and at an early day, through their influence, they became the scene of gracious revivals and the site of a thorough Presbyterianism.

Of the churches in these isles "Peter Heylin, D.D., chaplain to"—and we might almost add worshiper of—"Charles I. and

Charles II., monarch of Great Britain," thus writes:

"The isles of Guernsey and Jersey, the only remainder of the crown of England in the dukedom of Normandy, had entertained the Reformation in the reign of King Edward. But the Reformed religion, being suppressed in the time of Queen Mary, revived again immediately after her decease by the diligence of such French ministers as had resorted thither for protection in the day of their troubles. These French ministers, desiring to have all thing modeled by the rules of Calvin, endeavored by all the means they could to advance his discipline, to which they were encouraged by the brothers here and the Germans there. In pursuance of this plot, both islands joined in confederacy to petition of the queen for an allowance of the discipline, Anno 1563. They received a gracious answer. In the mean time the queen, being strongly persuaded that this design would advance the Reformation in those islands, was content to give way unto it in the towns of St. Peter's and Port St. Hillaries only, but no further. An authoritative letter was accordingly sent to those islands in these terms:

"'After our very hearty commendations unto you, whereas the queen's most excellent Majesty understandeth that these the isles of Guernsey and Jersey have anciently depended on the diocese of Constance, and that there be certain churches in the same diocese well reformed, agreeable throughout in the doctrine as set forth in this realm, knoweth therewith that they have a minister which ever since his arrival in Jersey hath used the like order of preaching and administration as in the said Reformed church, or as it is used in the French church of London, her Majesty, for divers respects and considerations moving her Highness, is well pleased to admit the same order of preaching and administration to be continued at St. Hillaries as hath been hitherto accustomed by the said minister; provided always that the residue of the

8

parishes in the said isle shall diligently put aside all superstitions used in said diocese, and so continue there the order of service ordained within this realm.' "

The same permission was also granted to the port of St. Peter's in the island of Guernsey. "In prosecution of which counsels the ministers and elders of both churches held their first synod in the isle of Guernsey on the 2d of September, Anno 1587, where they concluded to advance it by degrees in all the rest of the parishes, as opportunity should serve and the condition of affairs permit."

Thus, though the edict of Queen Elizabeth allowed the Presbyterian "preaching and administration" in one town only in each island, yet the "general plan was adopted by the decree of synods held under the countenance of the governors of Guernsey and the neighboring isles." In 1603, King James confirmed this permission and that to the whole island without limitation. This was their ecclesiastical polity in 1572.

Seeds of Presbyterianism proper were largely sown in England by distinguished champions of the Genevan discipline who from various causes took up their abode in the realm. In 1549, John a Lasco, on the the invitation of Cranmer, came to London to assist in the Reformation. He was a Polander of noble birth. Famous for his talents, his eloquence, his erudition and the purity of his life and character, he was welcomed everywhere, not by the learned only, but even by kings and princes. In Switzerland he visited Zwingle, and through his instrumentality was converted to God in Christ Jesus. In England he acquired very great influence. In 1550 a church of German refugees was established in London, and the church of the Augustin friars granted them as a place of worship.

This church, thus organized, was "erected into a corporation under the direction of John a Lasco, superintendent of all foreign churches in London, with whom were joined four other ministers, and as a mark of favor three hundred and eighty of the congregation were made denizens of England. The preamble to the patent sets forth that the German church made profession of pure and uncorrupted religion, and was instructed in truly Christian and apostolical opinions and rites." In the patent, solemn command is laid upon the "lord mayor, aldermen and magistrates of the city, and all archbishops, bishops and justices of the peace, to permit said superintendent and ministers to enjoy and exercise their own proper rites and ceremonies." Of which, poor Chaplain Heylin complains: "The inconveniences whereof were not seen at the first, and when they were perceived were not easily remedied." He further moans that they were greatly assisted by "Sir Francis Knollis," who among other misfortunes "had retired from Frankfort to Geneva, and did there contract acquaintance with these sore troublers of the pope's peace," Calvin and Beza and the rest of the consistorians, whose cause he managed at the court upon all occasions, having great influence as comptroller of the household.

Besides this church there arose in London another, composed of French Presbyterians. The establishment of this church was due, in part at least, as the sorely-grieved Heylin writes, to the influence of "Goodman Gillie, Whittingham and the rest of the Genevan conventicle, who repined and grudged at the Reformation (in England) because not fitted to their phancies and Calvin's platform." Through them we are left to infer a letter was secured from Calvin to Bishop Grindal begging that "by his countenance or connivance such of the French nation as had been forced by their conscience to flee into England might be permitted the free exercise of their religion. By whose solicitation the church of St. Anthony, not far from Merchant Taylors' hall, was assigned to the French, with liberty to erect the Genevan discipline for ordering the affairs of their congregations, and to set up a form of prayer which had no manner of conformity with the English liturgy." Alas! this "toleration of presbytery in a church founded and established by the rules of episcopacy could end in nothing but the advancing of a commonwealth in the midst of a monarchy."

Thus Presbyterianism in England had before its eyes for its instruction, encouragement and direction these large, strong and thoroughly-organized congregations.

Among the most remarkable eras in the history of English Presbyterianism was the five years' reign of the bloody Mary. The rod laid on the back of Puritanism by King Henry the Eighth was no pliant twig. But Mary, in her salutation to the people, when she put on the crown, said to them, "My father made your yoke heavy, and I will add to your yoke; my *little finger* shall be thicker than my father's *loins;* my father chastised you with whips, I will chastise you with scorpions." And she did! How thoroughly and terribly we may judge by the fact that during her brief reign some four hundred persons were publicly put to death in various ways, besides those who were secretly murdered in prison; "of these twenty were bishops and dignified clergymen, sixty were women, among whom some were big with child, and above forty were children." Even the bones of the eminent dead were dug up and *cited by the royal inquisitors to appear in court and answer charges against them, and then burned for non-appearance!* Verily, she chastised with scorpions!

Vast numbers, however, fled to the Continent, to France, to Geneva, to Basle, Frankfort, Emden, Strasburg, Dorsburg and Zurich, where they were received with all tenderness. Hundreds upon hundreds of these fugitives thus scattered themselves over continental Europe—bishops, deans, doctors of divinity, eminent preachers, noblemen, merchants, tradesmen, artificers and many also of the poor common people. In many of these places these people, learned and unlearned, clergy and laymen, became more fully acquainted with thoroughly-organized Presbyterianism. They were most hospitably entertained, and thus became well acquainted with those who had organized congregations, presbyteries and synods on the Presbyterian plan. They became familiar with the views of the great Presbyterian Reformers, and with the arguments by which those views were substantiated. They had now free access to the extant Presbyterian literature, to peruse, to study and to compare with Scripture at their leisure.

At the death of Mary and the accession of Elizabeth, in 1558, these exiles, clerical and lay, eagerly betook themselves to their English homes, many of them sorely impoverished, carrying back with them little but their new knowledge of religion and a zeal new kindled by persecution, and very many of them now thoroughly Presbyterian in their views of church polity. Inasmuch as that modern curiosity, High Churchism, was then unknown, very many of the preachers imbued with these principles were placed in the pulpits of the national church, and thus furnished with opportunities for the promulgation of Presbyterian views.

Various causes had conspired to empty the pulpits of the realm. A fearful disease had swept many of the incumbents to the grave, and the refusal of many more to submit to the queen's supremacy had left a large proportion of the parochial churches vacant. Hence, writes Heylin, "Such was the necessity which the Church was under that it was hardly possible to supply all the vacant places in it but by admitting some of the Genevan zealots to the public ministry. Private opinions were not regarded, nothing was more considered in them than zeal against popery, and their abilities in divine and human studies to make good that zeal.

"And if so many were advanced to places of note and eminence, there is no question to be made but that some numbers of them were admitted into country cures, by means whereof they had as great an opportunity as they could desire not only to dispute their Genevan doctrines, but to prepare the people committed to them for receiving such innovations, both in worship and government, as were resolved in time convenient to be put upon them."

The exiles had brought with them on their return numerous copies of the Genevan Bible, with its notes and comments, which formed another element in the powerful leaven working in the realm. Many of the returned preachers labored as they dared "with all diligence to bring the Church of England to a conformity in all points with the rules of Geneva. These, although the queen had laid by the heels" (Heylin, of course), "yet it is incredible how upon a sudden their followers increased in all parts of the kingdom, and this upon a double account; first, by the negligence of some and the connivance of other bishops, and partly by the secret favor of certain great men in the court." Among these were the earl of

Leicester, Lord North, Lord Knollis and Lord Walsingham, "who knew how mightily some of the Scotts lords and gentlemen had, in short time, improved their fortune by humoring their Knoxian brethren in the Reformation."

The *motive* is attributed by Heylin; the *fact* is all we need care for.

At length, in May, 1572, Parliament met and showed some disposition toward, if not a Puritan reform, at least a mitigation of royal rigors in dealing with the Puritans. To this Parliament leading Puritans addressed a treatise setting forth their grievances, presenting a platform for Church government, for the election of ministers, affirming their equality and specifying their duties, and pleading for the establishment by law of a discipline more consonant with the word of God and in agreement with that of the Reformed churches. The authors of this treatise presented it in person to the House of Commons, and were sent to prison for their pains. This tyrannous rejection of this petition resulted in the organization of the first English presbytery.

Situated on both sides of the river Wandel at its junction with the Thames, five miles from the general post-office in London, is the village of Wandsworth. Far enough from the court to be out from under the royal eye, near enough to be within reach of fraternal correspondence and sympathy with their friends in the city, this town was chosen by the Puritans as the place for effecting the proposed organization. At this place, on the 20th of November, 1572, assembled in strictest secresy a small body of ministers, with a considerable company of laymen, and organized a presbytery. Eleven elders were chosen, and their offices described in a register entitled the "Orders of Wandsworth."

Thus in the year 1572 we find a vast body of Presbyterians scattered through England, and besides the churches in the islands of Guernsey and Jersey, and the foreign churches in London, the English presbytery organized at Wandsworth.

SCOTLAND.

The moral and religious condition of Scotland just before the Reformation was such as to call a blush to the cheek of Rome, were it not that Rome's cheek had been long beyond the reach of a blush. Half of the wealth of the nation belonged to the clergy, and most of this half was in the hands of a few individuals. Ecclesiastics rivaled the nobility in magnificence and preceded them in honors. Inferior benefices were often put up for sale, or bestowed on the illiterate and unworthy minions of courtiers. The lives of the clergy were scandalously licentious. Monasteries covered the land, and were notoriously the haunts of lewdness and debauchery. The kingdom swarmed with ignorant, idle and luxurious monks who like locusts devoured the fruits of the lands. The people were sunk in profoundest ignorance. Under the teaching of their superiors they were thoroughly persuaded that the chief end of man, as a religious being, consisted in reciting *aves* and *credos*, attending upon the duties of the confessional, paying tithes, making offerings, paying for masses, going on pilgrimages, refraining from eating flesh on Fridays, and in doing whatever else was contrary to sound doctrines and to common sense.

Thus much had Romanism done to civilize and Christianize the people. Into this scene of infamy came Presbyterian Protestantism to scourge out the desecrators that made merchandise of the souls of men, to overturn the tables of the money-changers, and to turn the whole den of thieves into a house of prayer. The first beams of light penetrating this darkness came from Wickliffe, the morning-star of Reform. Early in the fifteenth century John Resby, a disciple of Wickliffe, came from England into Scotland, and popery burned him. Twenty-five years later came Paul Craw, a Bohemian disciple of Huss, preaching the truth, and he, too, soon found a martyr's grave. In 1528, Patrick Hamilton, of royal lineage and fine intellectual endowments, came home from his communings with Luther and Melanchthon, and lifted up his voice for Reform; and on the last day of February, James Beaton, archbishop of St. Andrews, burned him at the stake. Such was the effect of this atrocious murder upon the public mind that one said to the archbishop, still breathing out threatening and slaughter, "If your reverence will burn any more, it were well you did it in a cellar, for the smoke of Hamilton hath infected all it blew on."

But who can successfully oppose the mighty word of God, the fire and hammer that breaketh the rock in pieces, sharper than any two-edged sword, mighty through God to the pulling down of strongholds? The leaven had now been so long and powerfully working among the people, the hideousness of popery had now become so widely spread and the spirit of men so thoroughly aroused that in December, 1557, there was a grand coming together of the reforming lords and gentry of the realm at Edinborough, who formed and subscribed this bond:

"We, perceiving how Satan, in his members, the antichrists of our time, cruelly doth rage, seeking to downthrow and destroy the evangel of Christ and his congregation, ought, according to our bounden duty, to strive in our Master's cause even unto death, being certain of victory in him, the which, our duty being well considered, do promise before the majesty of God and his congregation that we, by his grace, shall with all diligence continually apply our whole power, substance and our very lives to maintain, set forward and establish his most blessed word of God and his congregation, and shall labor at our possibility to have faithful ministers purely and truly to minister Christ's evangel and sacraments to his people. We shall maintain them, nourish them and defend them, the whole congregation of Christ, and every member thereof, at our whole power, and expending of our whole lives again Satan and the wicked power that does intend tyranny and trouble against the aforesaid congregation. Unto the which holy word and congregation we do join us, and also do renounce and forsake the congregation of Satan, with all the superstitions, abominations and idolatry thereof, and moreover shall declare ourselves manifestly enemies thereto by this our faithful promise before God, testified to his congregations by our subscriptions at these presents. At Edinburgh, the third day of December, 1557 years, God called to witness."

This the first step toward formal organization of the evangelical forces is known as "THE FIRST COVENANT." It was signed by the earls of Argyll, Glencairn and Morton, Archibald, lord of Lorn, John Erskine of Dunn and a great number of distinguished men, who were thenceforth called the "lords of the congregation."

Rome responded to this protest by the martyrdom of Walter Mill, and the preachers responded to the martyrdom by passing through the land and preaching with new boldness and fervor the unsearchable riches of Christ.

Few Presbyterians from abroad visit the beautiful city of Edinburgh who do not also visit the venerable house which was the residence of several years of the Reformer Knox. It stands on the north side of High street, that memorable thoroughfare with the towering castle at the western extremity, and sloping down for a mile to the noted palace of Holyrood. It is a quaint, time-stained old pile of stone, irregular in its architecture, with narrow windows and outside stairway. It was in the narrow enclosure in the rear of this building that Knox was overheard praying, "O Lord, give me Scotland or I die." And it was in this house that Knox and a company of distinguished coadjutors were met in deep consultation on the memorable first of August,

1560. It was the day when Parliament was to assemble in the Tolbooth farther up the street. To this place of meeting the lords, now gathered at Holyrood, were to march in the solemn procession usually called "the riding of Parliament." "High street was already astir with multitudes eager to witness the spectacle, and congregating in groups, anxiously speculating on the probable issues of the meeting. The outward aspect of the crowds bore witness to scenes of recent warfare and lingering apprehensions of danger. The men were all armed, though not in uniform, each having armed himself with the weapons he could most readily procure, pikes, pistols, arquebuses or crossbows. Strangely picturesque must have been the scene as they marched about in this martial gear, with their long beards, voluminous coats and long flapping waistcoats."

By and by the noise in the streets drew the inhabitants to the windows to gaze on the spectacle. But among all the gazers few perhaps were filled with thoughts more solemn and emotions more profound than Knox and his associates. This Parliament was, under God, largely to affect the fate of the Reformation in Scotland. The eyes of Europe were fixed on that body. When it was organized, the all-important question of religion was introduced by a petition signed by many Protestants of different ranks, to the effect that "the anti-Christian doctrine maintained in the popish Church should be discarded, that means should be used to restore purity of worship and primitive discipline, and that the ecclesiastical revenues, which had been engrossed by a corrupt and indolent hierarchy, should be applied to the support of an active and pious ministry, to the promotion of learning and to the relief of the poor"—one-third for the support of colleges and schools, one-third for the relief of the poor and one-third for the support of the ministry. The petitioners held themselves ready to prove that those "who arrogated to themselves the name of clergy were destitute of all right to be accounted ministers of religion, and that from the tyranny which they exercised and their vassalage to the court of Rome they could not be safely tolerated and far less entrusted with power in a Reformed commonwealth."

In response to this petition a committee was appointed, consisting of Johns, Winraven, Spotswood, Willock, Douglas, Row and Knox, to draw up a confession of faith. In four days this body of men presented a confession in agreement with those of other Reformed Churches. The Protestant ministers were on the floor of Parliament to defend the confession if assailed. No opposition was made. Only two lords voted against it. In addition to the adoption of the confession this Parliament abolished the papal jurisdiction, prohibited under certain penalties the celebration of the mass, and rescinded all laws formerly made in support of the Roman Catholic Church and against the Reformed faith.

In connection with this external national Reform, measures were taken by the ministers to complete the work among the masses of the people. Leading ministers were distributed among the more important towns. But as the country parts were equally in need of ministers, and there was nothing like a sufficient number to meet the necessities of the case, the realm was divided into districts, and ministers appointed, with the title of superintendents, to see that the gospel was preached as widely as possible among the people.

This memorable year, 1560, was fittingly closed by the meeting of the first General Assembly of the Church of Scotland. This meeting was determined on by the Reformers, clerical and lay, soon after Parliament had abrogated Romanism in the realm and legalized Reform. On the 20th of December the Assembly met at Edinborough, and consisted of forty members, thirty-four laymen and six ministers. These six, however, were men of theological and ecclesiastical knowledge so ripe, of piety so pure and of influence so commanding as to leave no ground to fear either for the orthodoxy of the body in doctrine, or for the scripturalness of its measures with reference to church discipline. The same eminent men who had drawn up the confession of faith were appointed to frame a complete system of ecclesiastical government. For a pattern they looked as little to Geneva as to Rome, but away from both to the New Testament. When, after having spent much time in prayer, meditation and labor upon their work, they had brought it to a conclusion, they presented it to the General Assembly, by which it was amended and adopted, and has since been known as "The First Book of Discipline."

This book was too purely scriptural to be ratified by the privy council, but it was formally accepted and subscribed to by a large majority of its members. It provides for the minister or pastor to preach the gospel and administer the sacraments; the doctor or teacher to interpret Scripture, confute errors and instruct in theology; the ruling elder to assist the pastor in examining discipline and government; and the deacon to have special charge of the revenues of the church and the poor. These were the prominent officers of the church.

Besides these, the Book, to meet the exigencies of the times, provided for certain superintendents to travel from place to place among the regions destitute of the means of grace, to preach, plant churches and inspect the conduct of the less affluently qualified ministers in the country districts. It also provided for a class of laborers, termed exhorters and readers, who, though not fitted for the ministerial office, might yet do good service by visiting and giving instruction among the more ignorant of the population.

It further provided that the people should elect their own ministers. The affairs of each church were to be managed by the pastor, elders and deacons, who constituted the kirk session, and who were to meet as often, at least, as once a week. There were to be associations of ministers and elders, which soon became formal presbyteries. Above these were the provincial synods, and over all the General Assembly, composed of ministers and elders commissioned from different parts of the kingdom.

In June, 1563, the Assembly met and established, as writes Hetherington, "one of the most important principles of our existing system of church government." It was "statute and ordained" that *any person thinking himself* aggrieved by the sentence of the kirk session should have liberty to appeal to *the synod, and if necessary from the synod to the General Assembly.*"

The rapid growth of the Church in Scotland is seen in the fact that while the first General Assembly, in 1560, consisted of only forty members, and of these only six were ministers, and these six ministers formed fully one-half of all the Protestant ministers in the realm, at the meeting of the Assembly of 1567, seven years after the first, "the Church embraced two hundred and fifty-two ministers, four hundred and sixty-seven readers and one hundred and fifty-four exhorters, and this growth was in spite of incessant opposition on the part of those in power, "bent on the destruction of the Church by every artifice that craft and malice could suggest." Nor was the rigor of its internal discipline at all behind its external growth. "Offenders of every kind and degree were compelled to yield obedience to its sacred authority, noblemen and ladies of the highest rank submitted to its disciplinary censures, lordly prelates were constrained to bow their unmitred heads to its rebuke; over the refractory members of its own body its power was extended in the impartial administration of even-handed spiritual justice, and even the stormy tumults of a fierce and turbulent populace were often quelled and hushed into peace and silence at the utterance of its calm and grave command."

Thus the year 1572 found in Scotland a most complete, compact and thoroughly-organized Presbyterianism.

III.

THE CHAMPIONS.

HAVING now taken a rapid survey of the religious field three hundred years ago, let us set before our eye the chief champions on both sides who marshaled the hosts for conflict.

1. First and foremost among the leading antagonists of Presbyterianism then, as in every age, was the pope of Rome. The wearer of the triple crown at the opening of the year 1572 was Michele Ghislieri, *alias* Pius V. In sanctity this pope was, according to the Romish standard, next to immaculate, while in persecuting spirit he surpassed the ferocity of the American savage. His bull, *in cœna domini,* ordered to be read through all time, on every Thursday before Easter, in every parish church throughout the world, excommunicates all princes,

magistrates and other men in authority who in any way favor heresy or interfere with ecclesiastical jurisdiction, who appeal from the pope to a general council or who say that the pope is subject to a council. In February, 1569, Michele excommunicated Queen Elizabeth, absolving all her subjects from their oath of allegiance and consigning to perdition all who thenceforth submitted to her authority. He was in principle as bloody a persecutor as Nero or Diocletian. Among his proud, ferocious boasts was this: "I have no other object in life than that of suppressing heresy, and my efforts have received divine aid. I have converted many who departed from the faith; the bodies of certain men who were leaders in heretical opinions I have caused to be dug up and burnt." His injunction to the French butchers of Protestants was, "Take no Huguenot prisoner, but instantly kill every one who falls into your hands!" So enthusiastic was he in his admiration of the demon Alva that he sent him a consecrated hat and sword. On the first day of May, 1572, this one of the "chief monsters that plague the nations" passed to his account, and was succeeded on the 13th day of the same month by Hugh Buoncompagni, cardinal of St. Sixtus, who took the name of Gregory XIII.

One of the first acts of this pope was the promotion of his illegitimate son John to the cardinalship. He had become father to this son before he became cardinal, and in his office as cardinal he seems to have been much less profligate than the present bosom friend of Pope Pius IX., the notorious Antonelli. Closely connected with the Guises of France, he was inexhaustible in his expedients for the destruction of Protestantism, and it was under his eye that the jubilations over the massacre of St. Bartholomew were conducted.

2. Prominent among the willing instruments of the pope was Catherine de Medici. This woman was a child of a highly-distinguished Florentine family. She was the

daughter of Lorenzo de Medici and niece of Pope Clement VII. At the age of eleven she was left an orphan. Florence having revolted and expelled the creatures of the pope, he besieged it for eleven months. Catherine was then in a convent in the city, and so intense was the hatred of the Florentines toward his Holiness that the city council proposed to hang Catherine, his niece, in a basket over the walls that she might be a mark for her uncle's artillery. Well would it have been for her thus to have died and escaped the career of crime through which she passed to the grave!

Francis I. was now king of France. He had three sons. The second of these, Henry, was fourteen days older than Catherine. King Francis was in need of money; his son Henry was ready to take a wife. Lorenzo de Medici had his daughter Catherine, niece of the pope, and Lorenzo was ready to furnish the wife, and the pope the money, on condition that Francis would accept the two together. The alliance was galling to the pride, but grateful to the purse, of the king; and being then in no fear that Henry would become his successor on the throne, Francis reluctantly consented.

Catherine was overjoyed. "Now," she exclaimed, "I shall be daughter-in-law of the great king of France!" With a brilliant retinue she sailed for France, and the wedding was celebrated at Marseilles. Three years after, the king's oldest son was taken off by poison, and at length Francis died, an exhausted libertine, and Henry became king and Catherine queen of France.

This woman was very beautiful, of considerable talent, of boundless ambition, of fathomless cunning, deceitful above all things and desperately wicked. She paid assiduous court to the notorious Diana de Poitiers, mistress of her husband, and virtually queen of France. In 1559 her husband was killed in a tournament and their son Francis II. became king, and his beautiful young bride, Mary of Scotland, niece to the duke of Guise and the cardinal Lorraine, the queen.

Catherine now thought herself virtually queen, since the sovereigns were so young and the king so feeble, but she was sadly disappointed. The Guises at once took complete charge of the royal puppets and of the kingdom. Poor Catherine! But where there is a will there is a way. She now joined with the Huguenot leaders, and schemed to arrest and imprison the sovereigns and make way with the Guises, and thus come to power. This plot being discovered and brought to naught, she joined the opposite party, and did her utmost to induce the king to have Condé assassinated. Francis refused, and one of the Guises exclaimed in his vexation: "Now, by the double cross of Lorraine, we have a poor creature for a king!" But this royal obstacle was not allowed long to stand in the way. He died suddenly, and not without the horrid suspicion that his mother had a hand in the murder. By the death of Francis the poor sickly boy, Charles IX., became king and his infamous mother virtually dictator in the realm. "She now gave full swing to her atrocious genius. She first plunged her children into such a vortex of licentious pleasure that they were speedily divested of all moral sense," and thus ready instruments in any atrocity

Such, in 1572, was one of the chief organizers of the massacre of St. Bartholomew—niece of one pope, a willing tool of another and a ringleader in all schemes for ridding France of the professors of the religion of Jesus.

3. Next to Catherine, and co-operating with her as the most bitter foes of true religion three hundred years ago, were the Guises.

In 1527, Francis I. had made Claude, a son of the duke of Lorraine—an ancient province in the north-east of France—duke of Guise and peer of the realm. Of these Guises, in 1572, there were two upon the stage. One was Charles, brother of Mary of Guise, uncle to Mary queen of Scots and a cardinal, a cordial hater of the Reformed religion and plotter for its overthrow. A second, who took good care to leave no one in uncertainty as to his share in the work, was Henry, duke of Guise and nephew of the cardinal.

His father during the furious conflict of the times had been shot by a Protestant, and Henry had vowed bitter vengeance against the adherents of Protestantism. Restless, ambitious, full of intrigue, his ostensible zeal for religion was chiefly a cover for schemes for self-aggrandizement. This man was one of the leaders in the St. Bartholomew massacre.

4. Confronting these as the great champion of the truth in France stands the *admiral Gaspard de Coligny.*

His father had been made grand-marshal by Francis I., and he was present at the memorable interview between his king and Henry VIII. of England on the "Field of the Cloth of Gold." His mother was Louisa, sister of the proud constable Montmorency. He was born 1517, the year of Luther's theses at Wittenberg. Brave to recklessness, his stirring spirit was charmed with the perils of a hotly-contested battle. In an age of utter licentious levity he was grave and serious in thought and deportment. He was "thoughtful, cautious, devoted to a principle, suspicious of an impulse, directed by conscience and mindful of his responsibility to his king, his country and his God. His character was the material of which the serious Huguenot, Puritan and Covenanter were made. More like Cromwell than like Condé, he would have been at the head of the army what Calvin was at the head of the Reformed Church. The word discipline thrice given would have been his three rules of warfare. Success in battle he thought depended as much on obedience as upon courage; his mode was not to raise a yell, make a rush and sweep all before him; the living hurricanes should move according to laws. Although trained under his raving, swearing, mass-lipping old uncle, he went calmly to work and coolly finished it. A victory did not exalt him more than a defeat cast him down. Of all the Huguenot chiefs he was the lion-hearted, and neither wife nor comrade nor king could ever charge him with infidelity." Thus eloquently writes his American biographer, Dr. Wm. M. Blackburn.

The natural seriousness of Coligny's mind was deepened, the current of his thoughts turned toward objects loftier and more grand than those of camps and courts, and his character moulded for his future career as champion of the truth by the influence of his first wife, the beautiful and accomplished Charlotte de Laval, who was a daughter of Christ and the Reformation. His military genius was stimulated and fed by its prompt and emphatic recognition on the part of the king. "For your bravery everywhere," said the monarch to Coligny, "your superior discipline and your meritorious services at Cerisole and Boulogne, I confer upon you another rank of knighthood, the collar of my order, that of St. Michael;" and he soon added, "I appoint you colonel-general of the French infantry." In 1552 he was made by the king admiral of France.

But a yet higher promotion awaited him from the lip of the Captain of our salvation, and this through defeat, imprisonment and prostration on a bed of sickness. Philip II., with a vast and well-appointed army, was about to attack St. Quentin, and having taken this place, to advance on Paris. St. Quentin, a frontier town of Picardy, eighty-seven miles north-east from Paris, stood on a hill which sloped down to the river Somme. Around it was a broad ditch, and on three sides a marsh. Coligny determined to throw himself and his forces into the city. Between it and him lay the foe. His officers protested; Coligny persisted. With some seven hundred soldiers he outstripped the rest, cut his way through all opposition, and at midnight put the walls of the city between him and the besiegers, who at once swarmed around the city. He found the city walls tottering, its towers almost defenceless, with but little ammunition and some fifty muskets half fit for use. The scanty supply of provisions was husbanded. The women and children were shut up in the churches. The battle was fought under the walls, and lost, terribly lost. Coligny, surrounded by about eight hundred soldiers, saw from his watchtower the ruin of the French. In one hour the field was covered with the flower of the French soldiery and nobility weltering in their blood. Knowing, however, that by holding out he might detain the victors a while before its walls, and thus give Paris a breathing-time, instead of surrendering, he gathered the people and made them take an oath to behead the first man who should propose to surrender. He himself took the oath, pledging them his head if any of them should hear him speak the word surrender. For seventeen days the little band resisted, till, through eleven breaches made in the crazy walls by the cannonade, the foes swarmed in upon them. Coligny rushed into the thickest of the fight, and was taken wounded, but fighting hand to hand, and sent to prison. He lost St. Quentin, but saved France. And, more, himself was saved with great salvation. In prison he fell sick. During his convalescence he called for a Bible. On its pages he hung as a child on the words of a mother. God's words were found and he did eat them, and those words were to him the joy and rejoicing of his heart. His brother sent him books and opened the way for a correspondence with Calvin, who wrote to him, "I have heard that our heavenly Father hath so fortified you by the power of his Spirit that I should rather praise him for his kindness than urge you to greater efforts." Coligny was released from prison on paying a ransom. Resigning the government of Paris and the Isle of France, he sat down at the feet of his Christian wife for instruction in the deeper things of heart religion. One evening as he and she were gazing upon the starry heavens she said to him,

"How wonderful that you should have been so blest in your captivity!"

"Would you encourage me to remain firm, whatever might happen?"

"Indeed, I would," replied his helpmeet; "for though the trial of seeing you in prison for your faith would crush me, I would rather be crushed to nothing a thousand times than have you deny Christ."

"Enough. It was only for your sake that I thought of these terrors. As for myself, I have dwelt upon the joys of religion. What a delight to have a family altar, a chaplain in our castle, a church growing up in our town and a gospel preached to the poor!"

"And the joys beyond these," she answered, "the glories of the eternal heavens!"

Time rolled on. The kingdom was half Huguenot, this half embracing three-fourths of the men of letters. "Give me," said

Catherine to the admiral, "a list of your Protestant churches." He gave her a list of two thousand one hundred and fifty organized under regular pastors, besides many flocks of sheep without a shepherd. "How many troops can you raise?" she asked. "As many thousands as you wish," he answered.

Coligny had reformed his own family, had become the advocate of the Reformation in the realm, had presented the first example of godliness to the nobility of France when they were sunk in evil and immorality, and when wars arose he was made the Huguenot lieutenant-general.

This now was the man that filled the championship of the Church in France in 1572, and confronting him on the side of the papacy were the Guises and Catherine de Medici.

5. Like contrast of character meets us in passing from France into the NETHERLANDS in the persons of *Alva* and *William the Silent*.

The ancestors of William had for six hundred years been sovereigns of the duchy of Nassau, a patch of territory about half as large as the State of Rhode Island. His mother, Juliana, was a devoted Christian. His father was a true Protestant. Look at him as set before us by the graphic pencil of Motley: A Spanish cast of features, dark, well chiseled and symmetrical; his head small and well placed upon his shoulders; his hair dark brown, as were also his moustache and peaked beard; his forehead lofty, spacious, and already in 1555, when he was only twenty-two years old, prematurely engraved with the anxious lines of thought; his eyes full, brown, well opened and expressive of profound reflection. He dressed in the magnificent apparel for which the Netherlands were celebrated above all other nations.

We thus see him as Charles V. leaned upon him in the memorable scene of the abdication—that Charles who had put out of the world in various persecutions more than one thousand a year for every one of the fifty-five years of his life thus far—the princely page and the imperial persecutor.

It was a grand and most imposing scene. It was at Brussels, in the great hall of the ducal palace, October 25, 1555. The hall was hung with tapestry and festooned with flowers. At one end, under a royal canopy, was a platform, and upon it three gilded chairs. A vast and gorgeously-appareled assembly filled the hall. The clock has struck three. Charles enters leaning on William. He ascends the platform and seats himself in the central one of the three gilded chairs. He rises, leans on William and delivers his address of abdication. Thus the Netherlands passes into the grasp of the terrible Philip II.

In the providence of God, William is thrown into close connection with another tool of papal tyranny, Henry II. of France. The war between France and Spain closes in 1559 with the treaty of "Cateau-Cambresis," by the terms of which four nobles

WILLIAM OF ORANGE.

Page 157.

become hostages at the court of France. One of these four is William of Orange. King Henry is fond of the company of the handsome young prince. They go out to hunt in the woods of Vincennes. The king and the prince are alone together. The king has a grand project on his mind. He is communicative. William listens. "You know," says the king, "that heresy is increasing at a frightful rate in my realms and in Spain, and it may be in all the world. My conscience will never be easy nor my throne secure till I have rid my kingdom of these vermin. The king of Spain feels with me in this matter. We are now united, and we have resolved, by the blessing of Heaven, to blot out the very name of Protestants from our dominions." Philip in the Netherlands and Henry in France were soon to quench heresy in the blood of its abettors. Fine news this for the ears of the young Netherlander, the son of heretical parents! But he does not remonstrate, for it is William the Silent who is listening. But profoundly does he ponder the details of the fiendish plot. One lesson for the future champion of the truth of God!

A few days after this William requests leave to visit the Netherlands, and there uses all his influence with the authorities to have the Spanish troops, who were to have been the instruments in the work of death, removed from the country.

In 1567 a threatening insurrection broke out in Antwerp. Fifteen thousand Dutch Huguenots flew to arms. There was fierce talk of repaying Catholic oppression by pillaging their dwellings and churches. William saw nothing but disaster in the movement. He persuaded the Lutherans to take no part in the matter. Then he rode into the midst of the infuriated Huguenots, and by his eloquence and weight of character induced them to lay down their arms and disband. "But for his courage and prudence on this occasion millions of money and multitudes of human lives had been sacrificed."

Later in this year William withdrew with his family to Dillenburg, the ancestral seat of his family in Germany; tyranny had become too strong, and he preferred exile to slavery. Up to this time he had been nominally a Romanist, but his kindly nature revolted at papal cruelty, and papal power was now to crush all freedom, civil and religious. Now the bloody scheme whispered in his ear by the king of France in the forest of Vincennes was to be carried into execution. Here at Dillenburg he was led to deeper meditations on the nature of true religion. Here he became a pupil of the Holy Ghost. "It was about this time," writes Motley, "that a deep change came over his mind. Hitherto his course of life and habits of mind had not led him to deal very earnestly with things beyond the orld. The severe duties and the grave character of the cause to which his days were henceforth to be devoted had already led him to a closer inspection of the essential attributes of Christianity. He was now enrolled for life as a soldier of the Reformation. The Reformation was henceforth his fatherland, the sphere of his duty and his affection. The religious Reformers became his brethren, whether in France, Germany, the Netherlands or England.

"Hitherto he had been a man of the world and a statesman, but from this time forth he began calmly to rely upon God's providence in all the emergencies of life. His letters written to his most confidential friends, to be read only by themselves, and which have been gazed upon by no other eyes until after the lapse of nearly three centuries, abundantly prove his sincere and simple trust."

6. Face to face with this grand character in the fierce conflict of 1572 we find *Fernando Alvarez de Toledo,* DUKE OF ALVA.

Alva, "tall, thin, erect, with small head, long visage, lean yellow cheek, dark twinkling eyes, adust complexion, black, bristling hair and a long, sable, silvered beard descending in two wavy streams upon his breast. He did not combine a great variety of vices, but those he had were colossal, and he possessed no virtues. He was neither lustful nor intemperate, but his professed eulogists admitted his enormous avarice, while the world has agreed that such an amount of stealth and ferocity, of patient vindictiveness and universal bloodthirstiness, were never found in a savage beast of the forest and but rarely in a human bosom."

As a soldier he was inferior to no general of his age. As a disciplinarian he was second not even to Coligny. "He was more audacious, more inventive, more desperate, than all the commanders of that or any other age.

"As a financier he exhibited a wonderful ignorance of the first principles of political economy. No man before ever gravely proposed to establish confiscation as a permanent source of revenue to the State, yet the annual product of the escheated property of slaughtered heretics was regularly relied upon during his administration to replenish the king's treasury.

"As an administrator of civil and judicial affairs of the country, Alva at once reduced its institutions to a frightful simplicity. In place of the ancient laws of which the Netherlands were so proud, he substituted the *Blood Council.* This tribunal was even more arbitrary than the Inquisition. Never was a simpler apparatus for tyranny devised than this great labor-saving machine. Never was so great a quantity of murder and robbery achieved with such despatch and regularity. Sentences, executions and confiscations to an incredible extent were turned out daily with appalling precision.

"No mode in which human beings have ever caused their fellow-creatures to suffer was omitted from daily practice. Men, women and children, old and young, nobles and paupers, opulent burghers, hospital patients, lunatics, dead bodies,—all were indiscriminately made to furnish food for the scaffold and the stake. Men were tortured, beheaded, hanged by the neck and by the legs, burned before slow fires, pinched to death with red-hot tongs, broken upon the wheel, starved and flayed alive. Their skins, stripped from the living body, were stretched upon drums to be beaten in the march of their brethren to the gallows. The bodies of many who had died a natural death were exhumed and their festering remains hanged upon the gibbet, on pretext that they had died without receiving the sacrament. Women and children were executed for the crime of assisting their fugitive husbands and parents with a penny in their utmost need."

In 1572 this man is sixty-four years old. For four years he has filled the office of governor-general of the Netherlands. For forty-five years he has waded through blood. In six years he has ordered to death eighteen thousand six hundred human beings.

Well may Motley add that "the character of the duke of Alva, so far as the Netherlands are concerned, seems almost like a caricature. As a creation of fiction it would seem grotesque." This is the champion of the pope that in the Netherlands stood face to face with the large-hearted, tender-hearted Dutch Huguenot, William the Silent, in the great conflict three hundred years ago!

But Alva was only the tool—the right willing tool indeed—of another far away, whose mandates he most scrupulously obeyed—Philip II. of Spain.

7. *Philip II.* in person was "a small, meagre man, much below the middle height, with thin legs, narrow chest, and the shrinking, timid air of a habitual invalid." One of his eulogists writes of him, "His body was but a human cage in which, however brief and narrow, dwelt a soul to whose flight the immeasurable expanse of heaven was too contracted." He was in person greatly like his father, "the same broad forehead and blue eye, the same aquiline but better proportioned nose. In the lower

The Auto da Fe.

Page 165.

part of the countenance the remarkable Burgundian deformity was likewise reproduced. He had the same heavy, hanging lip, with a vast mouth and monstrously protruding lower jaw. His complexion was fair, his hair light and thin, his beard yellow, short and pointed. He looked habitually on the ground when he conversed, was chary of speech, embarrassed and even suffering in manner." In talents he was below mediocrity. "His mind was incredibly small."

How he stood affected toward the cause of truth may be learned in one characteristic incident in his life. It was the 18th of October, 1559. Philip had just arrived at Valladolid from the Netherlands. There were in the hands of the holy Mother Church thirteen heretics ready for sacrifice. In the great square was a huge pile of combustibles ready to be lighted. Present there were the king, his sister, his son, the high officers of the State, the foreign ministers and all the nobility of the kingdom, together with an immense concourse of soldiers, clergy and people. A sermon was preached by the bishop of Cuença, on what text we know not. At the close the inquisitor-general, Valdez, cried with a loud voice,

"O God, make speed to help us!"

Philip drew his sword. Then Valdez:

"Your Majesty swears by the cross of the sword whereon your royal hand reposes that you will give all necessary favor to the Holy Office of the Inquisition against heretics, apostates and those who favor them, and will denounce and inform against all those who, to your royal knowledge, shall act or speak against the faith."

The king answered,

"I swear," and signed the paper.

The fire was then kindled and the thirteen sufferers consumed. One said to the king, "How can you thus look on and permit me to be burned?" The king answered, "I would carry the wood to burn my own son were he as wicked as you."

These were the leaders in the Netherlands three hundred years ago—Philip II., Alva and William the Silent.

8. In England the one prominent figure is *Queen Elizabeth.*

As already remarked, the Reformation in England sprang from the hearts of the masses of the people, instructed from the Bible by their pastors and by the Spirit of God. For the great cause there no Luthers, Zwingles, Calvins, Colignys or Williams appeared. On the part of the Reformers were students here, writers of pamphlets there, and everywhere the hidden, hunted Christian people.

In opposition to these stood the queen of the realm. Elizabeth seems to have been an unhappy compromise between too little and too much. She possessed talents too large to allow her to resign herself and the government into the hands of her ministers, and too small to enable her to govern without them. Thus all their schemes were complicated with this unmanageable element, the queen's fancies and will. Changeful as the weather, irascible and petulant, she was to her ministers very much what a pet porcupine might be to a delicate lady. She was too shrewd to be largely or long deceived, yet schemes of the most delicate character and of momentous interest often had their fate bound up in a successful management of her caprices. Intensely self-willed, her one idol was the royal prerogative. Whatever she did in spite of the advice or with the consent of her ministers was dictated by its bearing on her prerogative. "She understood her prerogative, which was as dear to her as her crown or her life, but she understood nothing of the rights of conscience in matters of religion, and like the absurd king, her father, she would have no opinion in religion acknowledged, at least, but her own."

Destitute of conscience herself, how could she care for conscience in others? Charles I. lost his head for an arbitrariness of despotism no more flagrant than that of Queen

Elizabeth. Outstripping all legal enactment other than her own will, she, in 1567, sent her agents into the parishes, and gave orders that if the people neglected attendance upon the parish churches and frequented conventicles they should for the first offence be deprived of their freedom of the city of London, and after that be punished according as she should order. When Archbishop Grindal, who had gone to cruel lengths in enforcing the queen's mandates, at length hesitated and drew back, she was so enraged that by an order from the Star Chamber she confined him immediately to his house and kept him for six months from the exercise of his official duties.

With her Parliament she dealt just as summarily as with individuals. When motion was made in the House of Commons for an address to her Majesty, asking the release of certain members of the House from prison, the answer was, "that the House must not call her to account for what she did of her royal authority; that she did not like to be questioned, nor did it become the House to deal in such matters."

When Mr. Attorney Morrice moved to inquire into certain proceedings of her bishops, and the members proceeded to the discussion of the motion, this imperious woman sent for the Speaker, and bade him tell his fellow-legislators that this Parliament was called merely to enact sharp laws, to compel neglecters of her church service to attend upon it; that it was not meant that they should meddle with matters of State or causes ecclesiastical; that she was highly offended; that it was her royal pleasure that no bill touching any matters of State and causes ecclesiastical should be presented in the House. At the same time, Mr. Attorney Morrice was seized by the sergeant-at-arms, "discharged from his office in the court of the duchy of Lancaster, disabled from the practice of barrister-at-law, and kept for some years prisoner in Tutbury Castle." Thus in theory, and largely in fact, the government during this reign, lords, commons, legislature, executive and judiciary, consisted of one strong-minded woman.

As to theoretical religion, she was more a papist than a Protestant, and more an unbeliever than either. A *formal* papist her political situation forbade her to be; how could this female Henry VIII. submit to the pope in opposition to her predecessor, the male Henry VIII., her own father? Besides, her great men and a vast mass of her citizens would have interfered even at the expense of a revolution. On the other hand, if she hated Satan worse than she hated Puritanism, and especially Presbyterian Puritanism, the evil one was pretty well hated. The lord treasurer in the Star Chamber said, "The queen cannot satisfy her conscience without crushing the Puritans; she thought none of her subjects worthy of protection that favored innovations, or that directly or indirectly countenanced the alteration of anything established in the Church." Now, as the things established in the Church were her own arbitrary decrees, it is evident that, in 1572, England not only still had a pope, but already an infallible one.

Such being her theoretic notions about religion, no wonder if her personal piety was of a sort quite other than that enjoined in the New Testament. Indeed, in her passionate moods—and she not infrequently gave way to towering wrath—she could on occasion be as profane as any sailor in the royal navy. On a question between Bishops Ely and Cox this pious queen wrote to the latter in this mild strain: "Proud prelate, you know what you were before I made you what you are. If you do not immediately comply, by —— I will unfrock you!" It seems, then, that the bishop wore the frock and Queen Bess the trousers.

And yet she was distinguished by some very unmanly traits. "Her vanity," writes Froude, "was as insatiable as it was commonplace. No flattery was too tawdry to find a welcome with her; and as she had no repugnance to false words in others, she was equally liberal of them herself. Her entire nature was saturated with artifice. Except when speaking some round untruth, Elizabeth never could be simple. Her letters and her speeches were as fantastic as her dress, and her meaning as involved as her policy. She was unnatural even in her prayers, and she carried her affectations even into the presence of the Almighty."

To "gainstand," as Knox would say, this compound of imperious bigotry, impiety and overweening vanity, with her intense hatred of Puritanism, there were in England in 1572 only the great body of Bible students and the believers, some learned, many ignorant, some noble, many obscure, some wealthy, many very poor, praying in secret, stealing into conventicles, worshiping God in Jesus Christ with the sword ever gleaming in the air close to their heads.

9. In Scotland, in 1572, two towering champions confront each other—*John Knox* and the *earl of Morton.* There were not

wanting others of power and skill on either side, but without doubt these two were then the leaders in the field.

James Douglas, earl of Morton, had been one of the "lords of the congregation" who with others had signed the "First Covenant," pledging his life and substance to "the setting forward of the blessed word of God and his congregation." But having received considerable favors of the queen-regent Mary of Guise, the mother of Mary, afterward queen of Scots, he for a while vacillated between the contending parties, and seemed to be, as Sadler, the English envoy at the time, describes him, "a simple, fearful man."

At the death of the queen-regent, however, Morton emerged from this state of duplicity into the man he really was—bold, decided, self-willed and utterly unscrupulous. He was distinguished for licentiousness in his private life, for ability, avarice, rapacity and entire want of moral principle. Cognizant of the plot for the murder of

Darnley by Bothwell, he, though refusing to take part in it, yet gave no information whereby the crime might have been prevented; and when the deed was done, he was among those who subscribed a bond to protect Bothwell from the legal consequence of his crime, and he used every endeavor to secure the marriage of Mary with her murder-stained paramour. By his misconduct in public and private life he made himself so generally odious that when at length he was arrested, condemned to death and executed, there were few to mourn for him. The Catholics hated him for the part he had taken as a nominal Protestant, the Protestants for his want of principle, his vileness of character, and for the sore injuries he had inflicted upon the Kirk. He died, however, with a calm, undaunted spirit.

10. Face to face with this bad man stood one at length acknowledged almost by unanimous consent as from sandal to turban a true man, if there ever was one—JOHN KNOX.

On the coast of Fifeshire, some forty miles north-east from Edinburgh, on a small bay, the visitor finds the ruins of the old castle of St. Andrew's. There they show the tourist the horrid old "Bottle Dungeon." It is cut out of the living rock, one side of which is washed by the ever-restless sea. The opening in the top is circular and about seven feet in diameter. Below, it widens to twenty-five feet, and is of about the same depth. Down into this granite bottle the victim was lowered by a windlass, and there left to pine and starve, or to await the hour of execution. In imagination one may still hear the sighing of the prisoner and the moaning of those appointed to die. In an old tottering relic of the western wall of the castle they point still to the window out of which Beaton gazed in such content upon the burning Wishart, and out of which so soon he himself hung a ghastly corpse.

It was in this old castle that Knox, soon after the murder of Wishart, began to preach the gospel of the kingdom, and from this time till his death his name and character and personal influence were the life and soul of the Reformation in Scotland. Richly endowed with mental power, and with keen insight both of men and of the nature of the service to which the hour bade him, he was a true son of Issachar, with understanding of the times to know what Israel ought to do. Not even the sages of our American Revolution saw more clearly into the true relations between subject and sovereign than did this rough, vigorous Scotchman. In one of those noted interviews with Mary, the latter spitefully asked him, "Think you that subjects having the power may resist their princes?"

To this the Reformer answered, "If princes exceed their bounds, madam, no doubt they may be resisted even by power. For no greater honor or greater obedience is to be given to kings or princes than God has ordained to be given to father or mother. But the father may be struck with a frenzy in which he would slay his children. Now, madam, if the children arise, join together, apprehend the father, take the sword from him, bind his hands and keep him in prison till the frenzy be over, think you, madam, that the children do any wrong? Even so, madam, is it with princes that would murder the children of God that are subject unto them. Their blind zeal is nothing but a mad frenzy; therefore, to take the sword from them, to bind their hands and to cast them into prison till they be brought to a more sober mind, is no disobedience against princes, but just obedience, because it agreeth with the will of God."

"Thus spoke Calvinism," writes Froude, "the creed of republics in its first hard form."

Of this man this elegant and learned historian thus further speaks:

"John Knox became the representative of all that was best in Scotland. He was no narrow fanatic who in a world in which

God's grace was equally visible in a thousand creeds could see truth and goodness nowhere but in his own formula. He was a large, noble, generous man, with a shrewd perception of actual fact, who found himself face to face with a system of hideous iniquity. He believed himself a prophet with a direct commission from Heaven to overthrow it.

"Such was Knox, the greatest living Scotchman. The full measure of Knox's greatness no man in his day could estimate. No grander figure can be found in the entire history of the Reformation in this island. Cromwell and Burghley rank beside him for the work which they effected, but as politicians and statesmen they had to labor with instruments which they soiled their hands in touching. In priority, in uprightness, in courage, truth and stainless honor, the regent Murray and our English Latimer were perhaps his equals, but Murray was intellectually far below him, and the sphere of Latimer's influence was on a smaller scale. The time has come when English history may do justice to one but for whom the Reformation would have been overthrown among ourselves, for the spirit Knox created saved Scotland; and if Scotland had been Catholic again, neither the wisdom of Elizabeth's ministers, nor the teaching of her bishops, nor her own chicaneries, would have preserved England from revolution."

Of Knox the quaint Carlyle writes: "It seems hard measure that this Scottish man now should have to plead like a culprit before the world intrinsically for having been, in such a way as it was then possible to be, the bravest of all Scotchmen. Had he been a poor half-and-half, he could have crouched into a corner, like so many others. Scotland had not been delivered and Knox had been without blame. He is the one Scotchman to whom of all others his country and the world owe a debt. He has to plead that Scotland would forgive him for having been worth to it any million of unblamable Scotchmen that need no forgiveness. He bared his breast to battle, had to row in French galleys, wander forlorn in evils, in clouds and storms, was censured, shot at through his windows, had a right sore fighting life; if this world were his recompense, he had made but a bad venture of it."

11. Knox stood not alone indeed in Scotland in this memorable year. There were others on his side of whom the world was not worthy. Among these was a young man, twenty-seven years old this year, and an honor to the cause and his race. This was ANDREW MELVILLE. Weak in body, he was anything but weak in intellect and courage. He was distinguished as an Oriental scholar, familiar with law, and with the great principles of civil government. Master of a strong voice, a fluent elocution, a cogent, incisive diction, of great dialectic skill and of ardent spirit, he could so utter what he knew as not only to leave his hearers in no doubt as to his meaning, but also to work

conviction in even unwilling and prejudiced minds. His tone of spirit is shown in many a sparkling incident.

On one occasion, when a committee from the General Assembly, headed by Melville, waited on Morton as regent, the latter said that—

"The General Assembly was a convocation of the king's subjects, and that it was treasonable for them to meet without the king's permission."

"If this be so," answered Melville, "then Christ and his apostles must have been guilty of treason, for they called together great multitudes without asking permission of the magistrates."

Biting the head of his staff, Morton "growled in that deep undertone which marked his occasional fits of cold, ruthless anger:"

"There will never be quietness in this country till half a dozen of you be hanged or banished!"

"Tush, sir!" replied Melville; "threaten

your courtiers after that manner. It is the same to me whether I rot in the air or in the ground. The earth is the Lord's. I have been ready to give my life where it would not be half so well expended. Let God be glorified; it will not be in your power to hang or exile his truth."

No, Knox was not alone. There was Melville, and there were others with him. Nevertheless, the one towering form on the side of truth in Scotland in 1572 was that of John Knox.

There, then, is the wide field of conflict, reaching from Scotland to Piedmont, and there stand the great champions before us—the pope yonder, Queen Elizabeth here, between them Catherine and Coligny, William and Alva, Knox and Morton.

It only remains to glance at certain incidents in the actual conflict.

IV.

THE CONFLICT.

1. SCOTLAND.

IN SCOTLAND, in 1572, a war was waged with an earnestness and zeal that became the importance of the interests at stake. Romanism was pretty thoroughly paralyzed, but in the bosom of the Reform itself worldly and wicked statecraft was doing its utmost to hinder, hamper, cripple, corrupt and despoil the Church.

At the opening of this memorable and in many respects disastrous year, James VI. of Scotland, the son of Mary queen of Scots and the wretched Darnley, was eight years old. Mary, his mother, was prisoner in the grasp of Elizabeth, and the earl of Mar, weak rather than wicked, was regent.

The parties in the contest then waged were the Church on the one hand and a worldly, grasping court on the other, Knox leading the one, Morton the other. The question in controversy was the disposal of the Church revenues. The Reformation found the Church in possession of a large amount of property and a rich revenue flowing in therefrom. The Protestant nobility had cordially consented to and assisted in the abolition of papal jurisdiction; now the decision was to be made as to the disposal of these revenues. The demand of Knox and his party was that, while a certain portion might be allowed to the Romish bishops, abbots, priors and the like during their lifetime, the rest, and at the death of these incumbents their income also, should be appropriated, one portion to the support of the poor, another to educational institutions and a third to the support of the clergy. But the nobles looked with greedy eye upon these treasures, and under the lead of Morton plotted and schemed to direct the golden streams into their own coffers.

Accordingly, on the death of the popish archbishop of St. Andrew's, Morton obtained a grant from the privy council empowering him to dispose of the archbishopric and its revenue. Not daring, however, formally to hold the benefice in his own hands, he induced John Douglas, the rector of the University of St. Andrew's, to take the office and title, with the understanding that Morton was to have the lion's share of the income. Douglas, as archbishop, had also a seat in Parliament. Thus the way was open for the infliction upon the Church of a set of ungodly officers whose titles and duties were alike disallowed by Presbyterians, and for the diversion of the ecclesiastical revenues into avaricious hands.

Against this plan Knox loudly exclaimed, and the General Assembly sent a remonstrance to Parliament, denouncing the scheme, protesting against Douglas taking a seat in that body as lord-bishop, and threatening Douglas with excommunication. Morton's influence, however, prevailed. Through the influence of the Church the tithe-collectors of St. Andrew's refused to pay the money into the hands of Douglas. Then Morton secured a mandate from the regent forbidding their collection of these tithes. Erskine of Dun, however, prevailed with the regent to annul this prohibition. In his remonstrance upon this point Erskine deplores the "great disorder used in Stirling in the last Parliament in creating bishops, placing them in Parliament and giving them a vote in that body, in despite of the Kirk, and in high contempt of God, the Kirk opposing herself to that disorder."

But Morton was not to be baffled. That golden prize was too precious to be lost if there were any way to grasp it. The Kirk must be entrapped into the scheme. Accordingly, in January, 1572, an irregular and unauthorized convention of the superintendents and certain ministers assembled at Leith for consultation. Mistaking its own powers, this body appointed a committee to confer with the privy council, and agreed to ratify the conclusions they might reach in accordance with certain instructions. The result was a joint committee of six ministers and six of the council to settle affairs of national importance between Church and State. This abnormal, unauthorized committee agreed to the subtle scheme for setting up Mortonism in the Church, by which, under unlawful ecclesiastical forms, the patrimony of the Church might feed the greed of avaricious lords.

According to this scheme, the titles of archbishop and bishop were to remain, as also the bounds of the old popish dioceses, until the majority of the king (he was now eight years old) or until Parliament should determine in the matter, these dignitaries to be chosen by an assembly of learned ministers, to have like jurisdiction with the superintendents and to be subject to the General Assembly in spiritual and to the king in secular matters. Like arrangements were made respecting abbacies, priories and the rest, and the holders of the larger benefices to have place in Parliament.

Morton was victor. Ambitious ecclesiastics would now fill the offices, draw the revenues and pay over the chief share to the patrons through whose influence they found way into their high places.

The scheme soon received from the wits of the day the contemptuous name of Tulchanism. In the Highlands it was not uncommon to deceive refractory cows into giving their milk by stuffing the skin of a departed calf with straw and placing it beside the cow as her own offspring, and now the milkmaid had little difficulty in safely filling her pail. The name of this surreptitious calf was Tulchan. No sooner did the popular mind comprehend this new procedure than it saw in the diocese the cow, in the bishop the stuffed calf and in the patron the one who secured the milk. Hence these ecclesiastical tools were called *Tulchans.*

Morton's Tulchan, Douglas, was first ordained and installed archbishop of St. Andrew's, and Knox, being invited by Morton to assist in inaugurating Douglas, replied by anathematizing both Douglas and Morton.

In August the General Assembly met at Perth, and had barely the courage and good sense to protest that the Leith arrangement should be accepted merely as *ad interim* until further order be obtained from the king, regent and nobility. This was bowing before the storm, and the poor Church reaped a sad harvest from this unmanly cowardice.

Two other serious calamities came upon the Church—Knox died and Morton, the originator of Tulchanism, became regent. Mar, worn out with anxiety and toils, passed away, and Morton took the helm of the tossing, laboring, groaning ship of State.

But the greatest sorrow of all, as it at the same time deprived the Church of her Elijah and left in the hands of Ahab a ministry in the main timid and time-serving, was the death of Knox.

Long had he been sighing, "Call for me, dear brethren, that God will in his mercy please to put an end to my long and painful battle. For now, being unable to fight, I thirst an end before I be more troublesome to the faithful. God is my witness, whom I have served in the Spirit, in the gospel of the Son of God, that I have had it for my only object to instruct the ignorant, to confirm the faithful, to comfort the weak, the fearful and the distressed by the promise of his grace, and to fight against the proud and rebellious by the divine threatenings."

To Morton he said, "Well, God has beautified you with many benefits which he has not given to every man. And, therefore, in the name of God, I charge you to use all these benefits aright, and better in time to come than ye have done in times by-past. If ye shall do so, God shall bless you and honor you; but if ye do not, God shall spoil you of these benefits, and your end shall be ignominy and shame." I wonder if Morton thought of these words that day when at the old Tolbooth he lay with his neck on the block and the grim axe of "the maiden" descending upon it?

A vast concourse attended the funeral of Knox; and looking into his grave, Morton said, "There lies one who never feared the face of man." At Morton's execution his headless trunk lay till sunset of the day of his execution on the scaffold, and then, "covered with a beggarly cloak," was carried by common porters to the burial-place of criminals, unattended and unwept by those who in his prosperity had been his professed friends.

The close of the year 1572 left the poor Kirk in Scotland tossed from billow to billow on a wild, dark sea—Morton carrying it now according to his will with a high hand, the General Assembly and the good, faithful men paralyzed by their recent loss and overawed by the bold, bad regent, Morton.

2. ENGLAND.

In England the year 1572 was one of sore distress among the scourged believers in the truth. Over their prostrate forms the imperious queen rode in a heavy four-wheeled chariot.

Of the wheels of this chariot, one was her *Parliament.*

In those palmy days of the divine right of monarchs this body was much like a school of trembling urchins under the rod of a passionate mistress. When, in 1571, Strickland moved for further reformation, the queen's treasurer reminded him that "all matters of ceremonies were to be referred to the queen, and that for them to meddle with her prerogative was not convenient." The queen sent for Strickland and forbade him the Parliament house. In May, 1572, the lord-keeper charged Parliament in the queen's name, "See that the laws enforcing the discipline and ceremonies of the Church are put in execution, see and consider if others be wanting and so *gladius gladium juvabit;* the civil sword will support the ecclesiastical as beforetime has been used." When two bills of Reform had passed the House, the queen sent for the Speaker and demanded that the two bills be given up to her, and bade the Speaker to inform the House that it was her pleasure that no bills concerning religion should henceforth be received unless the same should first have been received and approved by the bishops or clergy in convocation. The servile Commons not only sent her the bills, but humbly begged that she would not conceive an ill opinion of the House if she did not approve of them. A member who ventured to grumble at this treatment was sent to the Tower.

Another wheel in this heavy chariot was the *Act of Uniformity.*

This act specified any number of minute rules of worship, and, as if this were not enough, the clause was added: "The queen is hereby empowered, with the advice of her commissioners or metropolitan" (the advising of Queen Elizabeth by any one was not unlike the advising of a wolf by a lamb), "to ordain and publish such further ceremonies and rites as may be for the advancement of God's glory and edifying his Church and the reverence of Christ's holy mysteries and sacraments."

Thus in reality one passionate, profane woman was constituted dictator in the Church of Christ. This act was abundantly hedged about with penalties. Whoever ventured to address his Maker in any other language than that thus prescribed was liable to the loss of goods and chattels for the first offence, to twelve months' imprisonment for the second, and to confinement during life for the third.

The third of these chariot wheels was the *Court of High Commission.*

The aim of this court was to bring the law to bear upon the citizen. The court consisted of men, mostly laymen, whose duty it was to go through the realm and execute the laws made way for in the Act of Uniformity.

The fourth wheel was the court called the *Star Chamber.* It was so called, it is said, from the gilt stars that glittered in the ceiling of the hall where the court used to assemble, the only stars that ever shone approvingly on either this body or its deeds.

This was a court composed of "certain noblemen, bishops, judges and counselors of the queen's nomination, to the number of twenty or thirty, with her Majesty at their head, *who is the sole judge* when present, the other members being only to give their opinion." Its determinations were simply according to the royal will and pleasure, which determinations, however, were made binding by act of Parliament. This court was a terror to the whole realm.

With such a queen, so armed and equipped for the execution of her one bigoted, tyrannous will, what could her opposers expect? "Many were cited into the spiritual courts, and after long attendance and great charges were suspended or deprived; the messenger of the court was paid by the mile; the fees were exorbitant which the prisoner must satisfy before he is discharged; the method of proceeding was dilatory and vexatious, though they seldom called any witnesses to support the charge, but usually tendered the defendant an oath to answer the interrogatories of the court; and if he refused the oath, they examined him without it and convicted him upon his own confession. If the prisoner was dismissed, he was almost ruined with the costs."

"If a godly minister," writes one complainant, "omit but the least ceremony for conscience' sake, he is immediately indicted, deprived, cast into prison and his goods wasted and destroyed; he is kept from his wife, and children and at last excommunicated."

To make sure work throughout the realm, there were appointed in every parish four or eight censor spies or jurats to take cognizance of all offences given or taken. These were under oath to take particular notice of the conformity of the clergy or parishioners, and to give in their presentments when required. So that it was impossible for an honest Puritan to escape.

The result was that many churches in London were shut up, and the country was plunged into distress. Many persons heard no sermon in years. Hundreds of people flocked around the church doors, which were closed against them, while their pastors wandered through the land in poverty and their families were reduced to beggary. The prisons, too—the horrible, filthy, pestilential dungeons—were filled to overflowing with men, women and children of "whom the world was not worthy."

In December, 1572, this petition was put into the hands of the earl of Leicester: "We were condemned, according to the Act of Uniformity, to one year's imprisonment, which we have now suffered patiently, besides four months' close imprisonment before our conviction; by this means we and our poor wives and children are utterly impoverished, our health very much impaired by the unwholesome savor of the place and the cold weather, and we are likely to suffer still greater extremities. We therefore humbly beseech your lordship, by the mercies of God and in consideration of our poor wives and children, that you will be a means to the most honorable privy council that we may be enlarged, or if that cannot be obtained, that we may be confined in a more wholesome prison." Another petition of like import was sent to the privy council, and another still in the names of the women and children.

Thus was it in "Merrie England" three hundred years ago. A profane and heartless queen with her Parliament, Act of Uniformity, courts of high commission and Star Chamber on the one hand, and on the other prisons full of starving, freezing men, women and children, sheep of God's pasture, and all over the land tens of thousands worshiping God in secret chambers, where any moment her Majesty's spies like hungry wolves might pounce upon them and hurry them before relentless, despotic courts, and thence to pestilential dungeons.

3. THE CONTINENT.

Passing to the Continent, we find the conflict fiercely raging chiefly in France and the Netherlands.

In Germany the moderate and peaceful Maximilian II. wore the imperial crown, and the empire nestled in religious quietude under the broad wings of the "Augsburg Concession." The only sounds of conflict which were heard within its borders were such as arose from the ordinary warfare between truth and error in the preaching of the gospel from hundreds of pulpits, and from the local struggles between individual friends and foes of the word of God.

In Switzerland, also, the cantons were pretty equally parceled out between the adherents of Rome on the one hand and the Reformation on the other, and among those mountains there dwelt a comparative religious peace.

Over the WALDENSES the clouds, big with the wrath of St. Bartholomew's Eve, extended their black, threatening wings. When that horrid massacre took place, orders were sent to Biraque, the governor of Saluzzo, to slaughter all the Protestants within his jurisdiction. Appalled at these sanguinary instructions, he called the chapter together; and while some were heartily in favor of proceeding to the work, a majority insisted that there must be some misconception or misrepresentation, and counseled delay. This delay saved the poor Waldenses of that province from a horrid doom, for the burst of indignant execration that thundered through the world against that awful deed made even Romanism shrink from concentrating upon itself the additional odium of this additional crime.

In November, 1571, the Waldensians of the valleys, dreading the sanguinary intolerance of Castrocaro, governor under the duke of Savoy, appointed representatives from their various communities to meet Bobi, in the valley of Luserne, and renew their league for mutual assistance against their oppressor. In this convention they solemnly pledged themselves that "when any one of their churches should be assailed all the rest would combine in assertion of their common rights; that no one should adopt any measure in such matter without consultation with the rest; that they would adhere as one man to the union transmitted them by their fathers and never abandon their religion."

Strange to say, there is a letter extant written to the duke of Savoy, in September, 1571, by that curious compound of weakness, duplicity and villainy, Charles IX. of France, in favor of the persecuted Waldenses.

But when the sounds of the St. Bartholomew massacre came shrieking and moaning through the gaps of the mountains, Castrocaro, catching the welcome scent of blood, exclaimed, "Sixty thousand Huguenots have perished in France, and do you, miserable handful of heretics, think you are to escape!" The papists around caught up the watch-word, and got ready for another bloody revel. The startled Waldenses began to prepare for the worst. The women and children sought the securest caverns in the upper mountains; the men, remaining behind, prepared their weapons for defence and set themselves to watch and pray.

But the outcry of horror which resounded through Europe at the assassinations in France took effect upon the duke of Savoy, nor was his heart untouched by the utterances of woe from the poor victims. He protested against the awful enormity, vowed that he would be participant in no such crime, and the savage Castrocaro was obliged reluctantly to sheath his sword.

Thus, while the year 1572 was one of apprehension and sometimes of terror among the Waldenses, it was not one in which they were called to resist unto blood.

4. THE NETHERLANDS.

In the Netherlands, however, the clouds everywhere gathered blackness, and the poor Dutch Huguenots were called to fresh woes. On the one side was William as the champion of the Bible; on the other, Alva as the champion of the Inquisition. William was weak, Alva was strong; William was mild, Alva was fierce and bloody. The story of the conflict of 1572 is a very simple one. It was merely aggression and merciless slaughter on the one hand, and, so far as William's orders prevailed, defence on the other. The contrast in spirit between the two parties may be seen in these two orders: to Diedrich Sonoy, his lieutenant-governor for North Holland, William wrote: "See that the word of God is preached, without, however, suffering any hindrance to the Romish Church in the exercise of its religion; restore the fugitives and those banished for conscience' sake, and require of all magistrates and officers of guilds and brotherhoods an oath of fidelity."

On the other hand, Alva's orders with respect to Zutphen, which had offered but a feeble resistance to his troops, were, "Leave not a single man alive in the city, and burn every house to the ground." Just about the opening of the year, Alva had sent two Italian assassins to England to poison or shoot Queen Elizabeth.

William was now in Germany attempting to secure means in men and money to carry on the war. But his eye was on, and his heart was in, and his influences powerful over, the down-trodden, struggling Netherlands. Brill was suddenly captured by Admiral de la Marck, never to be recovered by Alva. Flushing, too, was gained by the patriots. "The first half of the year 1572 was distinguished by a series of triumphs, rendered still more remarkable by the reverses which followed at its close. Nearly all the important cities of Holland and Zealand raised the standard of him whom they recognized as their deliverer. With one fierce bound the nation shook off its chain. City after city also in Gelderland, Overyssel and the See of Utrecht, all the important towns of Zealand, accepted the garrisons of the prince and formally recognized his authority." In these struggles, during William's absence and contrary to his will, deeds of terrible ferocity were enacted. The estates of Holland met at Dort on the 15th of July, elected William's tried friend, Paul Bruys, advocate of Holland, and resolved to raise the means for prosecuting the work of liberation from Alva, Philip and Rome.

By this assembly the prince was clothed with virtually dictatorial powers. Toward the end of July, William appeared on the field at the head of an army. The dawn of a bright day seemed to be gleaming in the sky. Coligny wrote him that he had succeeded in securing a promise from Charles IX. of a strong French reinforcement. But all at once, like a thunder-peal from a clear sky, came the news of the St. Bartholomew massacre. William was struck down, as he said, as with a blow from a sledge-hammer. The Spanish army was now besieging Mons, and William was just within striking distance when the awful news arrived. William was beaten and his troops butchered, he himself barely escaping capture and death. And now over the Netherlands rolled the wave of reverse and massacre. Mons capitulated. The gibbet was set up and an awful butchery began, and went on day after day, month after month. Mechlin fell, and for three days long the city was abandoned to that "trinity of furies, murder, lust and rapine, under whose promptings human beings became so much more terrible than the ferocious beasts." Zutphen fell; the whole garrison was put to the sword. The citizens were stabbed in the streets, hung on the trees in the parks, stripped naked and turned into the fields to freeze to death in the cold winter night. Five hundred were tied two and two, back to back, and drowned in the Yssel. Many were hung by the feet and left to die. Naarden fell, and "miracles of brutality were accomplished." Nearly the whole population, soldiers and citizens, were butchered. Men were slain and women outraged in the very churches and in the streets. Alva wrote: "They have cut the throats of the burghers and garrison, and have not left a mother's son alive."

William escaped from Mons with twenty horsemen and repaired to Holland. The year closed while the waves of war were raging about the walls of the devoted city of Harlem. Thus in the Netherlands the year opened with sunshine, passed into clouds and darkness and closed in blood. The condition of God's people during its latter months is written in the book of inspiration: "They were tortured, not accepting deliverance, that they might obtain a better resurrection: and others had trial of *cruel* mockings and scourgings, yea, moreover, of bonds and imprisonment: they were stoned, they were sawn asunder, were tempted, were slain with the sword:

they wandered about in sheep-skins, and goat-skins, being destitute, afflicted, tormented (of whom the world was not worthy): they wandered in deserts, and in mountains, and in dens and caves of the earth."

5. FRANCE.

In France the year 1572 opened under an apparently serene sky, and yet the angels saw that sky full of clouds and those clouds black with storm and death. The Huguenot population numbered millions, and the Huguenot leaders were strong, wise and brave. In 1570, under the lead of Coligny, they had secured a treaty granting them pardon for all past offences, declaring them capable of filling all offices, civil and military, renewing the edicts for liberty of conscience and ceding them for two years, as places of refuge and pledges of their security, Rochelle, La Charité, Montauban and Coignac. Thus the civil wars seemed to be ended, and the only contests awaiting the faithful those which were to be waged by the sword of the Spirit.

Besides this, the king of France had concluded a defensive alliance with England, which promised still greater security to the Huguenot cause. In this security there seemed to be, on the part of the Protestants, profound repose.

In addition to all this, the king of France had offered his sister Margaret in marriage to Henry, the young king of Navarre. After much hesitation the mother of Henry consented and came with her son to Paris, where the wedding was to be celebrated. She was received with great pomp and ceremony. The Huguenots, also, on invitation, flocked to Paris to attend the nuptials. As Henry was a Protestant, the son of a devotedly pious and ardently zealous Protestant mother, and Margaret was a papist, the event seemed significant of kindliest harmony in Church and State.

But underneath all this seeming brightness there lurked the profoundest treachery.

The Huguenots had been lured to Paris to a marriage feast; they found that the feast was preliminary to an awful slaughter. The idea of a general massacre of the Huguenots was anything but shocking to the papist mind of that day. Butcheries of the Waldenses and Albigenses and butcheries in the Netherlands had rather whetted than cloyed the Romish appetite for the blood of heretics. Philip of Spain and the pope of Rome were always ready for it. Who should bear the infamy of having first suggested this particular massacre is hardly known. It is attributed by some to the grand-master of the Inquisition at Rome, red as he was all over with the blood of the saints. But as to the willing agents in the work there can be little doubt. At the head of the butchers stands the grim form of Catherine de Medici. Side by side with her was Henry duke of Guise. His father, Francis, had been slain in his camp before Orleans by Poltrot de Meré, a Protestant. Henry chose to consider Coligny as the instigator of the murder, though both the character and solemn denial of Coligny removed all doubt from honest minds. But from this time "death to Coligny and the Huguenots" was the watchword of Henry of Guise.

Another bitter foe was the widow of the slain duke of Guise, Anne, now the duchess of Nemours, who, from being a Protestant, had become a fierce Romish bigot.

Another still was the king Charles IX., a man subject to fits of passion that bordered even on frenzy, and whom his mother knew well how to lash into fury.

This king, however, was rather the tool than the originator of the plot. Often he shrank with horror from the suggestion. But he lived in mortal dread of his mother, so familiar with poison and so deeply suspected of having poisoned his brother. Bitterly reproaching him for his reluctance, Catherine said to him, with tears and tones which were ever at her command, "Why this ingratitude to your mother? You hide yourself from me. You take counsel with my foes. You will make France a prey to the Huguenots. Either be guided by me or let me go back to my native country, that I may not witness such disgrace." The poor king was frightened, and begging his mother's pardon, promised obedience.

Many events foreshadowed the coming horror. In the rue St. Denis stood a huge cross commemorating the execution of three men, "principally because they had there celebrated the Lord's Supper." For this crime their house had been pulled down, and on the spot this cross erected as a warning to heretics. By the treaty of 1570 it was agreed that this memento of bloodshed should be removed. Its removal was ordered by the king, but the officer was deterred from obeying the order by fear of the mob. One dark night, however, the attempt was made. The attempt was discovered. The mob assembled. The cry "To arms!" was heard in the streets. There was a fierce riot, in which two houses were burned and a "sermoner" killed. At last the cross was removed to the cemetery of the Innocents. Another mob rushed through the streets, crying, "Kill the Huguenots!" Houses were pillaged and families were murdered. Such was the temper of the Parisian papists surrounding the Huguenots who had come to the marriage.

Another token of the coming woe: Jeanne d'Albret, queen of Navarre, a warm, devout Huguenot, who had brought her son Henry to Paris to wed the daughter of Catherine, died. It was said that poisoned perfumes had been sold her in a Parisian shop kept by "the queen's poisoner." Her dying words to her son were, "I command you to persevere in the faith in which you have been reared. Keep no men in your service who have no fear of God, and whose lives are scandalous. Beware of wicked women."

The report that the queen of Navarre had been poisoned spread like wildfire, and carried dismay into the bosoms of the Huguenot chiefs. Of the character of this queen even a Romanist could say, "Her heart overflowed with every virtue and quality that ennobles and elevates mankind." It was the ninth of June, 1572. At the funeral Henry rode at the head of eight hundred noblemen clothed in black, accompanied by troops of papists clad in scarlet.

The wedding was postponed, and through the streets were heard the ominous muttering, "See these accursed Huguenots, these outcasts of heaven, deniers of God, haters of the saints! Sing us one of your whining psalms!" Well does Blackburn say, "the Huguenots were walking on the sides of a volcano." Not a few of them, oppressed with a sense of coming ill, quietly slipped away to their homes.

The day for the wedding, the eighteenth of August, drew on. Coligny was at Chatillon, intending to be absent from the wedding. The king, however, begged him to come to Paris. As he mounted his horse a pious peasant-woman who had found Christ in the admiral's house seized the stirrup, clasped his knee and with entreaties and tears said, "Ah, my good master, if you go to that wicked court we shall never see you again." Then throwing herself at the feet of the lady of Chatillon, she cried, "He will never return. He will occasion, too, the death of more than two thousand others."

At last came the wedding-day. "Every spot of ground between the Louvre and the cathedral of Notre Dame was densely crowded. From every window and balcony the people gazed. King Charles, the Prince of Condé and Henry rode together, dressed alike as a sign of friendship. The men were in gorgeous apparel, the bride blazed in diamonds."

To his wife, about to become a mother, Coligny wrote: "To-day the king's sister was married to the king of Navarre. The next three or four days will be spent in banquets, balls, masquerades and tournaments. I hope to leave the city within seven days."

In the heart of Paris, on the northern bank of the Seine, stands that matchless architectural pile, the palace of the Louvre. Its eastern front, overlooking a broad street, is five hundred and thirty-eight feet in extent, and its sides on either hand reach westward five hundred and seventy-six feet. Across the street, opposite the eastern front, stands the church of St. Germain l'Auxerrois. Near this was the house of Coligny. Four days after the wedding, as the admiral was crossing the street between the Louvre and his own mansion, a shot was fired from a latticed window in the house adjoining the church, and two balls struck him, one taking off the first finger of his right hand, the other entering deep into his arm. Reeling back, he exclaimed, "I am wounded!" The cry arose, "The admiral is shot!" Pointing to the house, he said, "There is where it came from. Run tell the king!" The admiral was borne to his mansion, and soon it rang through Paris, "Coligny is slain!" Some exulted, some were filled with anguish, all looked with wonder to see what would follow. The crowd gathered, and some, dipping their fingers in the admiral's blood, called on God for justice. The Huguenot chiefs flew to Coligny's house, and one word from him would have unsheathed hundreds of blades to drink the blood of the Guises. This was what Catherine expected and desired. Let the Huguenots begin the work of death, and there will be good excuse for butchering them all.

Poor, half-crazy King Charles was playing in the tennis court when the word came, "The admiral is killed!" He threw down his racket and fell into one of those frenzies of raving and cursing that would have done credit to a demon.

Contrast the two scenes, separated only by the width of a street. In yon chamber lies the bleeding admiral, the surgeon having amputated his finger and cut the ball from his arm. "Nothing happens," he said, "but by the will of God. Why do you weep? I am happy in being thus wounded in

God's cause. Pray that he may strengthen me. I forgive with all my heart him who fired upon me and those who incited him. I suspect no one but the duke of Guise, and I am not even sure about him."

In a room in the Louvre, Catherine is closeted with Anjou, her wicked younger son. Charles enters, grinding his teeth and forcing between them a low, hissing growl. There they are, three wicked, shuddering souls! The door is flung open and the king of Navarre, Rochefoucauld and Condé enter. Condé holds up a blood-spotted hand and cries, "Justice!" "Whose blood is that?" cried Charles; "the admiral's?" And Charles poured out a stream of blasphemies fresh from the pit. "It shall be avenged," said Charles. "Guise is a villain. I will take vengeance on him so terrible that the child unborn will rue it."

The conspirators were at their wits' end. What to do next they did not know. There had been a blunder. An enormous crime had been perpetrated and nothing gained.

The admiral was still alive, the Huguenots exasperated and the mad king was raving at the conspirators.

Catherine and Anjou hid themselves in their closet, and the latter exclaimed, "Our noble enterprise has miscarried." It was Friday night, and all night long the lights gleamed in the Louvre, "as if the wicked who plotted against the just were afraid that God might come in the darkness." The question was how to kill the Huguenots.

Saturday came, and still the question was undetermined. A conclave was held in a house without the walls. Anjou, De Retz, Biraque, Tavannes and Nevers were there with Catherine. "The king must be frightened into the scheme," said Catherine. In due time the conspirators reappear at the Louvre.

The city that day was all in a tremble. There were muttered threats from the lips of half-armed soldiers, "low murmurs in dark alleys, the brag of street boys, prophecies of blatant women, quarrels at the markets and chaos everywhere." The Huguenots kept within doors, or if they walked out they watched for the dagger. Tidings now reached the ears of the Huguenots of "much carrying of arms to and fro, of pikes and lances secretly borne into the Louvre, rumbling of artillery wagons, forging of weapons, burnishing of armor, posting of soldiers, galloping of couriers," and every sign of awful preparation. If the devil ever spoke by the lips of man, it was when Anjou advised that *all Roman Catholics remove from the vicinity of the admiral's mansion that their places might be filled with the admiral's friends.* Coligny thought it very kind of the king. He did not see that the sheep were thus penned up for slaughter.

But the king must be gained. De Retz took him in hand. He said: "A great great danger threatens you. The admiral is a dangerous man. The effort to take his life was not made by Guise alone. Your mother and Anjou were with him. She saw how dangerous he was, and wished to rid the kingdom of the pest. It has failed, and the Huguenots will take up arms this very night." Charles, of course, went into a furious rage. And then Catherine opened her "budget of lies." She said, "I have intercepted their letters. They have sent beyond the Rhine for sixteen thousand men. They mean to place Henry of Navarre on the throne."

Charles doubted. A cold sweat stood on his brows. Catherine now asked, "Do you wish to be murdered? The Catholics will stand by you. They wish to end these wars at a blow." The king still hesitating, Catharine stung him with the suggestion that he was a coward. Goaded almost to madness, he sprang to his feet, raving like a madman; and bellowing forth his oaths, he exclaimed, "Hold your tongues! If you must kill the admiral, then kill all the Huguenots—all! all! Don't leave one to reproach me with the deed. Kill them! see to it at once. Do you hear?" Then rushing away, he left the conspirators to themselves.

They spent all that day and a good part of the night in arranging their plans.

Guise was summoned, and his uncle Aumale. "The city was divided into four districts. The general military superintendence was given to Tavannes. Montpensier had charge of the Louvre, *Guise the quarter of the admiral.* The hour was fixed. The signal would be given by the great bell on the Palace of Justice. The badge prescribed for the Romanists was a white badge on the arm and a white cross on the cap."

Guise now went out and spread enormous lies among the people: "The Huguenot chiefs were in revolt, and bringing in twenty-five thousand men to burn the city."

'Tis Saturday night. At dawn of the day when the loving Jesus rose from the dead the work of butchery will begin. There remained with Coligny the royal physician, .the chaplain pastor, Peter Merlin, Cornatou, Tolet, Le Bonne, five Switzers of Navarre's guard and a few servants. The last to leave him that night were his son-in-law, Teligny, and his faithful daughter Louisa. All was quiet in the mansion of the admiral.

Not so at the Louvre. After midnight Charles was pacing his room, shivering as one in an ague, the cold drops on his forehead, the agony in his heart. Catherine and Anne, widow of the duke Francis of Guise, all the conspirators, were there. "It is too late to retreat," said Catherine to Charles. "God never gave a man so fine an opportunity. If you delay, you will lose it." The trembling royal wretch sprang forward, laid hold of his cloak, and said with all his madness, "Well, begin!"

Guise withdrew. It was yet an hour and a half before the bell would ring. Catherine and her wretched crew clung to each other in silent horror. The dread of a prodigious, ghastly crime crushed their spirits.

It was not yet four o'clock. They could not wait. Catherine and her guilty crew on one side of the street, the wounded Coligny and his friends on the other, were startled by the tramp of cavalry and footmen. There was a crash at Coligny's door, a rush up the stairs, and shots and shrieks. Coligny had been lifted out of bed, and was praying with Pastor Merlin. The door of the room was dashed open.

"Are you the admiral?" demanded the assassin.

"I am," replied the old man. "But you, young man, should respect my gray hairs, and not attack a wounded man."

A curse and a thrust of a sword to the hilt into the admiral's heart was the reply.

The impatient, guilty Guise from the pavement below called out, "Behm, have you finished?"

"It is over," answered Behm.

"Throw him down;" and soon the body fell upon the pavement. A lantern was held near, and the blood was wiped from the face, when Guise said,

"Yes, it is he. I know him well. Lie there, thou serpent!" and he gave the hardly dead body a kick. Then the head was cut off and sent over to Catherine.

"Well done, my men," said Guise; "we have made a good beginning."

And now that the "good beginning" had been made, the work must go on. The king may repent, and that bell on the Palace of Justice will not ring for three-quarters of an hour. "Go," said Catherine, "and ring the bell in the church of St. Germain l'Auxerrois;" and the booming of that bell "unbarred the gates of hell."

When the bell rang, the king and his mother were looking from the windows of the palace upon the balmy Sabbath morning. "The weather," said Charles to his mother, "is rejoicing over what we are about to do."

At the signal the crowds rushed into the streets, and pistol shots and shouts and screams filled the air. The excitement of the moment filled the king with a frenzy, and grasping a gun, he fired into the crowd, crying, "Kill! kill!"

The soldiers had a list of the Huguenot

houses and lodgings. They broke down the doors and slew and ravaged and pillaged. The dawn now came and showed them their victims. "If one shut the door in the face of a ruffian, or refused to inform on his neighbor, or begged for his life, or wore not the white badge, or would not join in the slaughter," he was a heretic and was killed.

"Every rioter, every low villain, every malcontent, every menial greedy for plunder, every profligate, put on the white cross and became a volunteer. The populace became one vast mob; while dukes and lords were killing at the Louvre, the bands of the sections, men, women and even children, strove which should be first in the pious work. All Catholic Paris was at the business. Through street, lane, quay and causeway the air rang with yells and curses, pistol-shots and crashing windows; the roadways were strewed with mangled bodies; the doors were blocked with the dead and the dying. From garden, closet, roof or stable crouching creatures were torn and stabbed; boys practiced their hands at strangling babies in their cradles, and headless bodies were trailed along the trottoir. Carts struggled through the crowd, carrying the dead in piles to the Seine."

"Imagine a vast city in which sixty thousand men armed with pistols, stakes, cutlasses, poignards, knives and other bloody weapons are running about on all sides, blaspheming and murdering all they meet. The pavements were covered with dead bodies, the doors, gates, entrances of palaces and private houses steeped in blood; a horrible tempest of yells and murderous cries filled the air, mingled with the reports of firearms and the piteous shrieks of the slaughtered, the dead bodies falling from the windows, the court of the Louvre red with blood and the Seine running crimson!"

There was a full week of rioting and murdering. To sanction and stimulate the work, Rome wrought a miracle at noon on that awful day. A hawthorn bush in the "Cemetery of the Innocents," which had not bloomed for four years, now suddenly, out of season, by aid of a cunning friar, was covered with white blossoms. The king, court, council, clergy and all the rest of the murderous rabble went in procession to the cemetery to refresh their pure eyes with a sight of the miracle.

"See," said they, "the white cross triumphs!"

On their way the friars killed Huguenots and the monks cried out, "The Church revives by the death of heretics!"

The king, now fully in the spirit of the revel, gave orders for conducting the massacre. Eight hundred Huguenots were torn from the places in which they had sought refuge, led to a spot on the banks of the Seine called the "Vale of Misery," where they were shot or made to walk the plank into the river.

The headless body of Coligny was dragged about the streets, put over a fire and scorched, thrown into the river, taken out again, dragged about the street again, and then hung upon the gallows by the feet. His head, there is reason to believe, was sent to Rome to feast the eyes of the infallible. His castle was despoiled, the trees rooted up, the property confiscated, his family declared ignoble and all possible terrors heaped upon his children. His wife was at length seized, thrown into prison at Nice, persecuted and tormented for nearly twenty-seven years, until she was driven to madness and death.

Nor was the tide of massacre restrained within the walls of Paris. It flowed in one wave of blood, fire and war over France. Almost every village had its festival of blood. Nor was its duration limited to a day or a week. "For two months this horrible tempest swept over France, being more or less bloody according to the temper of those in authority." At Bourges, Rouen, Nevers, Toulouse, Bordeaux, Lyons, Orleans, Treves, the slaughter was immense.

The number of victims of this truly Romish exploit it is impossible to tell. "At

Paris the number may have been six thousand, in France fifty thousand," though some say seventy thousand, and others one hundred thousand.

The news of this piece of demonism filled the Protestant world with horror. The queen of England clothed herself in mourning and spurned the apologies of the French envoy with contempt. Knox in Scotland said to the French ambassador, "Go tell your master that God's vengeance will never depart from him nor his house, that his name shall remain an execration to posterity, and that none proceeding from his loins shall enjoy the kingdom in peace except he repent." The prediction was more than fulfilled. But how was the story of this enormity received by Rome and Romanism? At Madrid there was unbounded joy. Philip even laughed—an astonishing phenomenon in his life. He "seemed more delighted than with all the good fortune or happy incidents which had ever before occurred to him."

"In the Spanish camp before Mons the joy was unbounded. With anthems in St. Gudule, with bonfires, with festive illuminations, roaring artillery, with trumpets also and with shawms, was the glorious holiday celebrated in court and in camp." In Rome the bells rang, the bonfires blazed, the guns of St. Angelo thundered. The man who brought the precious tidings received a thousand crowns. The pope and cardinals marched in procession to the church of St. Louis, where Lorraine chanted the *Te Deum.* The pope sent to Charles IX. the golden rose. He had a medal struck, on one side of which was a destroying angel, the cross in one hand, a sword in the other, slaying heretics, and on the other a likeness of his Holiness, with the legend *Hugonottorum Strages*, 1572. He also had three frescoes painted in the Vatican, one representing the attack on the admiral, another the king in council plotting the deed and a third the massacre itself.

V.

CONCLUSION.

THUS was it with Presbyterianism three hundred years ago, and well were it for us all were we more familiar with the thrilling, bleeding, glorious tale. Well were it for our Church could our youthful Presbyterians be induced to fill their minds with the records of those days that so sorely tried men's souls, with the true character and history of our glorious Presbyterianism, with the heroism to which it gave birth, the heroes that glorify its progress and the services it has rendered the world. More than once it saved the Reformation in Britain, and once at least it saved free constitutional government from overthrow.

How instructive, too, and in many respects how cheering, is the contrast between those days and ours! Over all the round world, almost, no hindrance to the free propagation of the unsearchable riches of Christ.

> "From Greenland's icy mountains,
> From India's coral strand,
> Where Afric's sunny fountains
> Roll down their golden sand,
> From many an ancient river,
> From many a palmy plain,
> They call us to deliver
> Their land from Error's chain."

An active response to this world-wide call is forbidden by no satanic Catherine de Medici, by no blood-seeking Alva, by no imperious self-willed Elizabeth. Through all the changes of three centuries but one sturdy opponent of the truth remains unchanged in spirit, though wondrously changed in power, and that is the Roman papacy. By the blasphemous decree of infallibility, which assures us that the pope, issuing his edicts *ex cathedrâ* upon the subjects of morals and religion, cannot err, all the past enormities of the papacy, its edicts of blood and woe, are solemnly appropriated to itself and sealed as the infallibly righteous decrees of God. Not from innate bloodthirstiness, not from natural delight in persecution to butchery and flame, but simply as a duty to the truth, to the Church and to God, would the Romish apostasy, had it the power to-day, repeat the bloody work in any and every land. But, thanks be to God! the lion is gone into senility, his teeth are drawn and his claws are out, and hence there remains to him only the harmless privilege of bemoaning the palmy days of St. Bartholomew and wishing in vain for their return.

Since those days Presbyterianism has passed through many sore trials, has in some countries sadly betrayed its trust, but, withal, it has won many a notable victory.

On the subject of the present English-speaking Presbyterianism we quote the eloquent Dr. Blakie of Edinburgh:

"The career of English-speaking Presbyterianism may be said to have commenced in 1560, when the first General Assembly of the Church of Scotland met, under Knox, and numbered six ministers and thirty-four laymen. Three hundred years ago the English language was almost confined to England and the Scottish Lowlands, and the people who spoke it might fairly be estimated at five millions. That handful has increased to about seventy-five millions, and wherever the language has gone Presbyterianism has gone also. The six ministers of 1560 have as their successors in Scotland alone three thousand ministers. In Ireland there are about six hundred ministers and congregations. In England there are at least two hundred and fifty. In the Dominion of Canada there are upward of five hundred ministers and churches of our order. In Australia, New Zealand, Africa, West Indies, etc. there are about five hundred more. All the Presbyterian churches in the United States put together number about seven thousand two hundred. The Presbyterian churches that look back to the assembly of Edinburgh, in 1560, as their mother assembly, number in all about twelve thousand ministers and churches, living in the British Isles, in the United States, in British America, and in the isles of the southern seas. With the exception of the ten or twelve per cent. that constitute the Established Church in Scotland, the whole of this body owes its support to the freewill-offerings of the people, and therefore possesses at least the kind and degree of life and activity necessary for continuing its own existence. No political revolution can greatly affect its strength or its welfare."

May God add his blessing and imbue the Presbyterianism of the world with the orthodox fidelity of the Waldenses, with the prayerful zeal of Knox, as on his knees in the enclosure behind his house in High street he prayed, "O God, give me Scotland, or I die!" and with the purity, dignity and nobility of character illustrated in Admiral Coligny, and with the generous, tolerant spirit of William the Silent! Amen!

www.ingramcontent.com/pod-product-compliance
Lightning Source LLC
LaVergne TN
LVHW050513100826
845148LV00002B/326